A Book Of

FINANCIAL MARKETS & BANKING OPERATIONS

FINANCIAL MANAGEMENT SPECIALIZATION

M.B.A. : Semester – II [Course Code 205 FIN : No. of Credit – 03]

CHOICE BASED CREDIT SYSTEM AND GRADING SYSTEM

As Per New Syllabus, Effective from June 2019

Prof. Ameya Anil Patil

M.B.A. (Finance), B.E. (Computer), NET, SET

CAIIB, Lean Six Sigma Green Belt,

PGDIB, Ph. D. (Pursuing)

Assistant Professor (BBA, BBM-IB), SKNCC, STES, Pune

N4786

Financial Markets and Banking Operations　　　　　**ISBN 978-93-89825-76-3**

| **First Edition** | : | **January 2020** |
| **©** | : | **Authors** |

Published By :
NIRALI PRAKASHAN
Abhyudaya Pragati, 1312, Shivaji Nagar
Off J.M. Road, Pune – 411005
Tel - (020) 25512336/37/39, Fax - (020) 25511379
Email : niralipune@pragationline.com

➢ DISTRIBUTION CENTRES

PUNE

Nirali Prakashan : 119, Budhwar Peth, Jogeshwari Mandir Lane, Pune 411002, Maharashtra
(For orders within Pune)　Tel : (020) 2445 2044, Mobile : 9657703145
Email : niralilocal@pragationline.com

Nirali Prakashan : S. No. 28/27, Dhayari, Near Asian College Pune 411041
(For orders outside Pune)　Tel : (020) 24690204 Fax : (020) 24690316; Mobile : 9657703143
Email : bookorder@pragationline.com

MUMBAI

Nirali Prakashan : 385, S.V.P. Road, Rasdhara Co-op. Hsg. Society Ltd.,
Girgaum, Mumbai 400004, Maharashtra; Mobile : 9320129587
Tel : (022) 2385 6339 / 2386 9976, Fax : (022) 2386 9976
Email : niralimumbai@pragationline.com

➢ DISTRIBUTION BRANCHES

JALGAON

Nirali Prakashan : 34, V. V. Golani Market, Navi Peth, Jalgaon 425001, Maharashtra,
Tel : (0257) 222 0395, Mob : 94234 91860; Email : niralijalgaon@pragationline.com

KOLHAPUR

Nirali Prakashan : New Mahadvar Road, Kedar Plaza, 1st Floor Opp. IDBI Bank, Kolhapur 416 012
Maharashtra. Mob : 9850046155; Email : niralikolhapur@pragationline.com

NAGPUR

Nirali Prakashan : Above Maratha Mandir, Shop No. 3, First Floor,
Rani Jhanshi Square, Sitabuldi, Nagpur 440012, Maharashtra
Tel : (0712) 254 7129; Email : niralinagpur@pragationline.com

DELHI

Nirali Prakashan : 4593/15, Basement, Agarwal Lane, Ansari Road, Daryaganj
Near Times of India Building, New Delhi 110002 Mob : 08505972553
Email : niralidelhi@pragationline.com

BENGALURU

Nirali Prakashan : Maitri Ground Floor, Jaya Apartments, No. 99, 6th Cross, 6th Main,
Malleswaram, Bengaluru 560003, Karnataka; Mob : 9449043034
Email: niralibangalore@pragationline.com
Other Branches : Hyderabad, Chennai

niralipune@pragationline.com | www.pragationline.com
Also find us on 🄵 **www.facebook.com/niralibooks**

Preface ...

It gives me immense pleasure to present this book on 'Financial Markets and Banking Operations'. The book depicts the financial system in the country with regards to its several components and functions. Money market and Capital market, which are vital for provision of finance to trade and industry, have been discussed in detail. Special emphasis has been made to Banks and NBFC, and their functioning.

I am grateful to Mr. Jignesh Furia for presenting me with this wonderful opportunity to reach the student community. This book has been designed to fulfill the new syllabus requirements of M.B.A. : Semester II students.

I would like to thank Mr. Amol Mahabal for putting together the myriad sections in this book and thereby, presenting this book in a systematic way.

I would also like to thank Mrs. Yojana G. Deshpande and Mr. Ravindra Waldore for their valuable help in preparation of this book.

Finally, I express my deep regards towards Sinhgad Technical Education Society for providing me an enabling and supportive environment for learning and teaching.

Suggestions for improvement of this book are always welcome.

– Prof. Ameya Patil

Syllabus ...

1. Basic Concepts of Indian Financial System

Structure and Components : Indian Financial System in India, Role of Financial System in Economic Development. Introduction to Financial Institutions – Banking – Non-banking Institutions. Role and Functions of banks and their contribution to Indian Economy. Introduction to Financial Markets, Functions and Classification Money Market, Capital Markets, Bond Markets, Commodity Markets, Money Markets, Derivatives Market, Futures Market, Foreign Exchange Markets, Cryptocurrency Market. (7 + 2)

2. Money Market

Structure and Components : Participants in Indian Money Market Instruments, Structure of Money Market, Role of Central Bank in Money Market; Players in Indian Money Market, The Reforms in Indian Money Market. (7 + 2)

3. Capital Market

Components and Functions of Capital Markets, Primary and Secondary Market Operations, Capital Market Instruments, Preference Shares, Equity Shares, Non-voting Shares, Convertible Cumulative Debenture (CCD), Fixed Deposits, Debentures and Bonds, Global Depository Receipts, American Depository Receipts, Global Debt Instruments, Role of SEBI in Capital Market. (7 + 2)

Types of Banks and NBFCs : Central Bank, Nationalized and Co-operative Banks, Regional Rural Banks, Scheduled Banks, Private Banks & Foreign Banks, Mudra Bank, Small Finance Banks, Specialized Banks, NBFCS. Types of Banking : Wholesale and Retail Banking, Investment Banking, Corporate Banking, Private Banking, Development Banking. (7 + 2)

Accounting in banks, Electronics Banking, RTGS, ATM, MICR, OCR, OMR and DATANET, Petty Cash, Electronic Clearing Service (ECS), National Electronic Funds Transfer (NEFT) System, Real Time Gross Settlement (RTGS) System, IMPS. (7 + 2)

Contents ...

Chapter 1

Basic Concepts of Indian Financial System

Contents ...

Learning Objectives...

After studying this chapter, the student should understand:

1.   Concept of Financial system.

2.   Structure of Financial system – Financial Institutions, Financial Markets, Financial Instruments & Financial Services.

3.   Role of financial system in economic development.

4.   Financial Markets - Primary Market & Secondary Market, Money Market & Capital Market.

5.   Financial Institutions – Banking & Non Banking Institutions.

6.   Banks and their functions.

7.   Contribution of banks to Indian Economy.

8.   Concept of Bond markets.

9. Commodity markets and its benefits.
10. Concept of Derivatives markets.
11. Futures and Options.
12. Foreign exchange markets along with its structure, functions and types.
13. Concept of Crypto-currency market with special reference to Bitcoin.

1.1 INTRODUCTION TO FINANCIAL SYSTEM

- A country's financial system consists of its banks, securities markets, pension funds, mutual funds, insurance companies, market infrastructures, central bank, as well as various regulatory and supervisory authorities.
- These institutions and markets provide a framework for carrying out financial transactions and implementing monetary policy.
- They help to efficiently channel savings into investment, thereby supporting economic growth.
- The financial system is the most important institutional and functional vehicle for economic transformation.
- The aim of the financial system is to supply funds to various sectors and activities of the economy in ways that promote the optimum utilization of resources .

Definitions:

> **(1) Howells and Bain :** *"A financial system is defined as a set of markets for financial instruments, and the individuals and institutions who trade in those markets, together with the regulators and supervisors of the system".*
>
> **(2) Van Horne :** *"Financial system is defined as the purpose of financial markets to allocate savings efficiently in an economy to ultimate users — either for investment in real assets or for consumption"*

- Financial system thus, consists of a set of closely held financial institutions, intermediaries, financial instruments, financial services, methods of operations and procedures.
- It allows the transfer of money between savers and borrowers.
- It helps in the formation of capital, and meets the short term and long term capital needs of households, corporate and the Government.
- A financial system thus provides a mechanism by which savings are transformed into investment.
- It also consists of a set of rules and regulations, through which different financial instruments such as stocks & bonds are traded, and their prices determined.

- A financial System can also be defined as a set of Institutions, Instruments & markets which channels savings to their most efficient use.
- The basic function of the financial system is to enable transfer of financial resources (money or monetary instruments) from surplus areas to deficit areas, which is technically referred to as 'Financial Intermediation'.
- A well developed, efficient and effective financial system is essential for a strong economy.
- A financial system is efficient when there exists an Efficient Monetary System and Efficient Financial Markets for appropriate allocation of funds, and financial institutions like banks which will enable the mobilization of financial resources.
- In other words, the financial system mainly stands on three factors, viz. Money, Credit and Finance.
- Financial System of any country consists of financial markets, financial intermediation, financial instruments and services.

1.2 ROLE OF FINANCIAL SYSTEM IN ECONOMIC DEVELOPMENT

- A healthy and a sound financial system facilitates economic development of a country.
- A financial system provides several functions that aid economic development as outlined below:

1. **Financial Intermediation :**
- Financial systems perform the essential economic function of channelling funds from surplus units in the economy to deficit units in the economy.
- The channelling of funds from surplus areas (savers/lenders) to deficit areas (spenders/ borrowers) is very important because:
(a) Savers, with excess of available funds will have profitable investment opportunities for investing their excess funds.
(b) On the other hand, borrower/spenders will now get funds for investment.
- For example, a large corporation requiring funds for huge investments such as establishing mobile towers can get funds from public through issue of equity shares or debentures.

2. **Payment Mechanisms :**
- The financial system provides a variety of payment mechanisms for individuals and corporate such as cheques, debit cards ,internet banking, credit cards and many more.

3. Risk Transfer:

- Financial systems provide mechanisms for risk transfer.
- For example, insurance contracts allow a party such as a corporate or household to transfer the risk of loss of wealth due to fire or theft or other damage to another party such as an insurance company in return for a regular premium.
- In this way, risk is transferred from risk-averse entities to risk-takers.

4. Mobilization of Savings :

- Funds are mobilized from the savers or surplus units such as individuals, corporate, public sector units, Governments for Borrowers (e.g. issuers of bonds).

5. Financial Inclusion :

- A financial system helps in promoting the process of financial deepening and broadening.

6. Encourage Investments :

- A sound financial system will wipe out fear from savers and so they will convert their savings into investments.

7. Link :

- It serves as link between Savers and Investors.

8. Productive Investment :

- It channelizes the flow of savings into productive Investments.

9. Capital Formation :

- A sound financial system facilitates the purpose of capital formation in an economy by bringing together the supply of savings and the demand for investible funds.

10. Facilitates Price Discovery :

- The interaction between savers and borrowers facilitates price discovery for different financial assets through the forces of demand and supply.

11. Conversion of Savings into Investment :

- The system collects savings from households & facilitates its distribution for industrial investment.

12. Information :

- It provides the detailed information to various players in the market such as individuals, corporates, Governments and creditors to help them decide on future investment opportunities.

13. Standard of Living and Well-being:

* Existence of a sound and well organized financial system promotes the well being and better standard of living of the citizens.

14. Entrepreneurship Development:

* Financial market makes necessary financial resources available to the entrepreneurs, required for developing their business venture.

1.3 STRUCTURE OF FINANCIAL SYSTEM

* A organized Financial System is made up of the following components:
1. Financial Institutions,
2. Financial Markets,
3. Financial Instruments ,and
4. Financial Services.

1. Financial Institutions:

* Financial Institutions perform the function of financial intermediation, i.e. they channelize funds from individuals and corporate with surplus funds to those entities (individuals, corporate, government)desiring funds but have shortage of it.
* Financial Institutions includes financial intermediaries like banks, finance companies, insurance companies, mutual funds, pension funds, co-operative societies etc. as well as the financial regulators.

2. Financial Markets:

* Financial markets are a medium through which people can trade (buy and sell) financial securities.
* These financial securities can be stocks, bonds, commodities such as precious metals or agricultural goods.

  Example: New York Stock Exchange, Bombay Stock Exchange, MCX, Callmarket, U.S. Treasury's online auction site for its bonds etc.
* Thus, funds are moved from people who have an excess funds to people who have investment opportunities and lack of funds.
* Financial markets thereby, act as a facilitating organization and link between saver & investor.

3. Financial Instruments :

* They are also known as Financial securities.
* A financial instrument is a formal obligation that entitles one party to receive payments and/or a share of assets from another party.
* For example, loans, stocks and bonds are financial instruments as these instruments represent a claim on the future income/assets of the issuer/borrower.

- Financial instruments are a financial liability for the issuer/borrower and financial assets for the saver/lender.
- This financial claim is packaged in the form of a certificate, receipt or any other legal document.
- For example, share certificates and FD receipt.
- These documents act as a legal proof for the investor.
- PPF, KVP, loans, equities are different financial instruments.

Characteristics of Financial Instruments:

(a) Liquidity (quick conversion into cash).
(b) Collateral (security for obtaining loan).
(c) Price fluctuations of a financial security such as shares, bonds.
(d) Can provide Tax benefits.
(e) Easy transfer of instruments.

Classification of Financial Instruments :

- Financial instruments can be classified as, Debt and equity instruments.

(a) Debt Instruments :

- These instruments promise the payment of given sums to the investor.
  Examples : Bills and Bonds.
- Bonds represent debt owed by the issuer to the investor.
- On bonds, issuer normally pay periodic interest (called as coupon payments) until the maturity date and also pays the face value (par value) on maturity date.

(b) Equity Instruments :

- Equity represents claims to shares in the net income and assets of a firm.
- They represent ownership/voting rights.
- They do not have a maturity date.
- They are riskier than debt instruments.

4. Financial Services :

- Financial services bridge the gap between lack of knowledge of investors about financial instruments and markets.
- These are the services provided by financial institutions.
- Some of these services are as follows :

(a) Credit Rating,
(b) Deposit Insurance,
(c) Factoring and forfeiting,

(d) Syndicated Loan,

(e) Portfolio Management,

(f) Depository,

(g) Lease financing,

(h) Book building.

1.4 STRUCTURE OF INDIAN FINANCIAL SYSTEM

- As any matured Financial system, Indian financial system consists of following:

1. Financial Institutions,   2. Financial Markets,

3. Financial Instruments,   4. Financial services,

5. Financial Regulators.

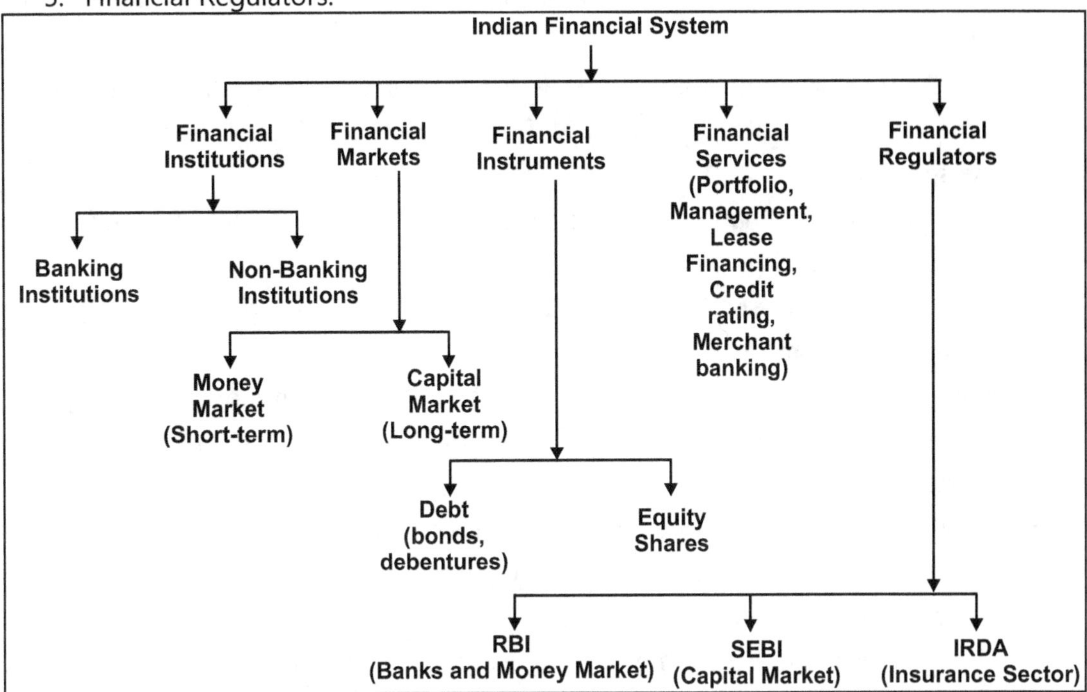

Fig. 1.1 : Structure of Indian Financial System

1. Financial Institutions (in India) :

- Financial institutions are classified as banking and non banking financial institutions.

- Banking institutions are creator of credit while non banking financial institutions are purveyors of credit.

- In India, non banking financial institutions namely the Development Financial Institutions (DFIs) and Non Banking Financial Companies (NBFCs) as well as Housing Finance Companies (HFCs) are the major institutional purveyors of credit.

2. Financial Markets (in India) :

- Money market and capital market are the organized financial markets in India.
- Money market is for short-term securities while capital market is for long-term securities.
- Primary market deals in new issues while the secondary market is meant for trading in outstanding or existing securities.
- There are three main sets of entities depending upon securities market.
- The corporate and governments raise resources from the securities markets to meet their needs of investment and the households invest their savings in the securities.
- The Central Government and the State Governments nowadays finance about two third and one third of their fiscal deficits respectively through borrowings from the securities market.
- Corporate sector finances about one third of its external finance requirements through the securities market.
- The household invest about six per cent of their financial savings in securities

3. Financial Instruments :

- Financial instrument is a claim against a person or an institution for the payment at a future date a sum of money or a periodic payment in the form of interest or dividend.
- Financial instruments may be primary or secondary securities. Primary securities are issued by the ultimate borrowers of funds to the ultimate savers e.g. Bank Deposits, Mutual Fund Units, Insurance Policies, etc.
- Financial instruments help the financial markets and the financial intermediaries to perform the important role of channelizing funds from lenders to borrowers.
- Both debt and equity instruments of varied features and characteristics are available in India.

4. Financial Services :

- Financial services include merchant banking, leasing, hire purchase, credit rating etc.
- Financial services rendered by the financial intermediaries' bridge the gap between lack of knowledge on the part of the investors and increasing sophistication of financial market and instruments.

5. Financial Regulators :

- Regulators are meant to ensure smooth and orderly working of the financial markets.
- In India, different financial markets have specialised regulators, viz.;

(a) Securities and Exchange Board of India (SEBI) – Capital markets,

(b) Reserve Bank of India – Banking sector and money market,

(c) IRDA – Insurance sector.

1.5 FINANCIAL INSTITUTIONS

Introduction :

- These are the entities between the ultimate borrowers and ultimate lenders.
- Financial Institutions perform the function of financial intermediation, i.e. they channelize funds from individuals and corporate with surplus funds to those entities (individuals, corporate, government)desiring funds but have shortage of it.
- Financial Institutions includes financial intermediaries like banks, finance companies, insurance companies, mutual funds, pension funds, co-operative societies etc.
- Financial regulators such as RBI (which regulates banks), SEBI (which regulates capital markets) and IRDA (which regulates insurance sector)in India are also a part of financial institutions

Banking Institutions and Non-banking Financial Institutions:

- Financial institutions are classified as banking and non banking financial institutions.
- Banking institutions are creator of credit while non banking financial institutions are purveyors of credit.
- Banks or 'Banking institutions' mainly provide services related to deposit of money and lending of money.
- They accept deposits from the public(depositors) and make loans to borrowers.
- Deposits include savings deposits, fixed deposits.
- Loans include term loan, cash credit, educational loan, vehicle loan, mortgage loans etc.

- Now, some commercial banks also provide various other financial services such as Insurance, Mutual fund units, Factoring, Demat account and hence, are referred to as 'Universal banks', wherein all these services are provided under one roof.
- In India, non-banking financial institutions namely the Development Financial Institutions (DFIs) and Non Banking Financial Companies (NBFCs) as well as Housing Finance Companies (HFCs) are the major institutional purveyors of credit.

1.6 BANKS

Introduction

- In India, banking is as old as ancient Vedic times.
- There were bankers known as Sheth, Shah who were carrying out the function of bank.
- Bank is a place where citizens of a country can place their hard-earned money in a safe and secured manner and in addition earn an interest on this money (Deposits).
- Also they provide an avenue from where businesses and individuals can get the money (finance) that they require .
- A bank is a financial intermediary which accepts deposits from surplus areas and loans out these funds to deficit areas. For example, a salaried person will have certain savings after satisfying his daily needs.
- Businesses may require finance for their expansion and modernization activities.
- The bank here will accept deposits from these salaried people and lend this money to business house.
- In most countries in the world, banks are regulated, either, by the government or central bank. For example, Indian banks are regulated by RBI (Reserve Bank of India), which is the Central Bank in the country.
- Popular banks in India are SBI (State Bank of India),BOB (Bank of Baroda), ICICI, HDFC and others.

Functions of Bank

- The banks perform financial intermediation by pooling savings and channelizing them into investment, which ensures continuance of an economy's growth engine.
- Banks have evolved from providing traditional services such as deposits and loans to provide services such as insurance, demat accounts and other fee based services.

- Below diagram gives a snapshot of various functions of bank.

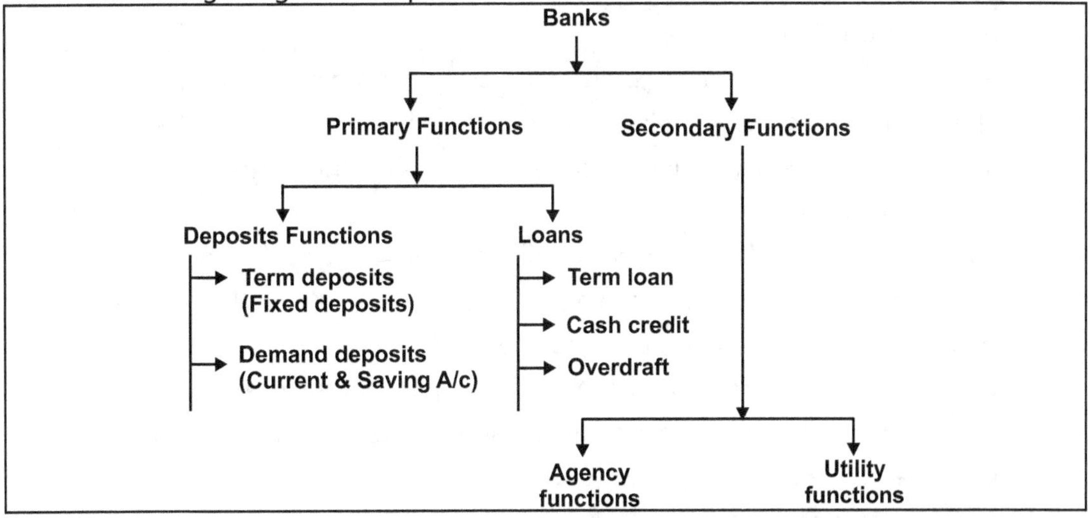

Fig. 1.2 : Functions of Bank

- Functions of bank can be broadly divided into primary functions and secondary functions .

(A) Primary functions

1. Accepting Deposits:

- Mobilization of the deposits from the public is the most important function of banks.
- A bank accepts money from the people in the form of deposits which are usually repayable on demand (demand deposits) or after the expiry of a fixed period (timed deposits).
- Banks act as custodians of public money.
- Traditionally, Indian banks have been offering four types of deposit accounts namely, Current Accounts, Saving Bank Accounts, Recurring Deposits and Fixed Deposits.
- However, due to competitive pressures, banks have introduced new deposit products, which combine the features of above two or more types of deposit accounts such as automatic sweeps and flexi FD.

2. Granting Loans and Advances:

- A bank lends out money in the form of loans to those individuals and business houses who require it for different purposes.
- A loan is simply a debt provided by one entity to another entity at a certain rate of interest.

- This money is actually a part of deposits which a bank lends after satisfying the minimum capital requirement.
- Granting loans and advances is also referred to as Credit.
- The main earnings of a bank is the interest from their customers (i.e. borrowers). So, it is very essential to lend money to the public through various products of loans and advances.
- For a specific period of time, banks will generally charge a higher rate of interest from the borrowers as compared to the rate of interest they offer to depositors, as bank is also an organization that exists for profit.
- Different type of bank loans basically differ in terms of their tenure and purpose.
- Generally, for all bank loans, securities and collateral have to be provided by a borrower to the bank.

(B) Secondary Functions :

1. Agency Functions:

- Agency functions are undertaken by the bank on behalf of the customers.
- Some important agency functions of bank are as follows :

(a) Payment and Collection of Cheques, Bills and Promissory Notes :

- Cheques, bills and promissory notes are negotiable instruments, which means they are written documents by which a right is created in favour of some person.
- The term negotiable instrument" is thus a written document transferable by delivery.
- As per Negotiable Instruments Act, 1881,"A promissory note is an instrument in writing containing an unconditional undertaking, signed by the maker, to pay a certain sum of money to or to the order of a certain person, or to the bearer of the instruments."
- Maker is the person who makes the promissory note and promises to pay.
- Payee is the person to whom the payment is to be made.
- As per Negotiable Instruments Act, 1881, A bill of exchange is "an instrument in writing containing an unconditional order signed by the maker, directing a certain person to pay a certain sum of money only to, or to the order of, a certain person or to the bearer of the instrument".
- As per Negotiable Instruments Act, 1881, A cheque is "a bill of exchange drawn on a specified banker and not expressed to be payable otherwise than on demand".

- So the payment and collection of these negotiable instruments is handled by a bank on behalf of its clients.
- Local and outstation cheques and bills of exchange are collected by the banks through clearing house facilities provided by the central bank.

(b) Execution of Standing Instructions :

- A customer may authorise his bank for the payment to various persons or institutions via use of standing instructions.
- These standing instructions are usually given in respect of periodical payments such as insurance premium, rents, subscriptions, donations and others.
- Bank, being an agent of the customer, follows these standing instructions.

(c) Acting as a Trustee, Executor :

- The bank also acts as trustee or executor for its customers to manage trust property as per instructions of property owners.
- As services of this kind require specialised knowledge, the bank discharges this responsibility more efficiently as compared to other agencies.

2. General Utility Functions :

(a) Safe Custody and Safe Deposit Vaults :

- Banks accept customer's valuables, jewellery, ornaments, documents, deeds or securities etc. for safe custody.
- They provide safe deposit vaults like lockers for storing these valuables.

(b) Remittances of Funds:

- Banks provide facilities for the transfer of money to any place within and out of the country.
- The funds are transferred by means of draft, telephonic transfer, electronic transfer such as internet banking, RTGS, NEFT etc.

(c) Pension Payments:

- Pension payments in the country are disbursed through banks.

(d) Acting as a Dealer in Foreign Exchange :

- Banks deal in foreign exchange, as they are authorized dealers.
- This enables the importers and exporters to obtain foreign currency in exchange of their home currency and vice-versa.
- Also, individuals can obtain benefits like payments for travel abroad, foreign education through these services of bank.

- Permission from the central bank is required for a bank to be able to deal in foreign exchange.

(e) Letter of Credit :

- Most international transactions are made through Letter of credit issued by the bank.

(f) Underwriting of Securities :

- The bank gives an undertaking that, if the shares issued by a company remain unsubscribed, the banks will subscribe them.

Banks and Economic Development:

- Commercial banks play a crucial role in the economic development of a country.
- They are the largest source of finance for capital investments in a country.
- They mobilise the savings for capital formation.
- They lend money to businesses for their projects, which in turn generate employment, accelerate economic activity in the country.
- Several infrastructure projects such as railways, roads, bridges, malls have been built thanks to the finance provided by commercial banks such as SBI,IDBI Bank, Bank of India and others.
- They also finance agricultural and related activities in the country.
- The commercial banks help the economic development of a country by appropriately following the monetary policy of the central bank.
- Thus the commercial banks contribute to the growth of an economy by granting loans to agriculture, industrial activities, trade activities by helping in physical and human capital formation and by following the monetary policy of the country.

Contribution of Banks in Economic Development :

1. Credit Creation :

- This is the most important function of commercial banks.
- For this purpose, they accept deposits and advance loans on credit to customers.

2. Capital Formation:

- Commercial banks mobilise the savings of people and these savings are effectively allocated to investors for productive investment.
- Thus, savings of people result in capital formation which forms the basis of economic development.
- Thus, commercial banks transfer funds from surplus areas to deficit areas.

3. Provision of Finance :

- Commercial banks are a very important source of finance and credit for trade industry and agriculture.

4. **Trade Finance :**
- Commercial banks provide finance to domestic trade as well as international trade.

5. **Promoting Balanced Regional Development :**
- Commercial banks open branches in rural and backward areas to provide credit facilities to the rural people.
- The funds collected in developed regions may be channelized for investments in the under developed regions of the country, so as to develop them.
- Thus, banks promote balanced regional development.

6. **Consumer Loans :**
- Commercial banks provide credit for purchase of consumer durables like T.V., refrigerator, vehicles etc., which are out of reach for some consumers due to their limited paying capacity.
- In this way, a demand is created for such consumer goods, which increase consumption in the country and thereby accelerate economic growth.

7. **Finance Employment Generating Activities:**
- Commercial banks do so through educational loans and providing finance to entrepreneurs for establishing their businesses.

8. **Transmission of Monetary Policy:**
- The commercial banks help the economic development of a country by appropriately following the monetary policy of the central bank.

1.7 FINANCIAL MARKETS

Introduction to Financial Markets :

- Financial markets are a medium through which people can trade (buy and sell) financial securities.
- These financial securities can be stocks , bonds, commodities such as precious metals or agricultural goods.

  Example: New York Stock Exchange, Bombay Stock Exchange, MCX, Callmarket, U.S. Treasury's online auction site for its bonds.
- Thus, funds are moved from people who have an excess of available funds and lack of investment opportunities to people who have investment opportunities and lack of funds.
- Financial markets thereby, act as a facilitating organization and link between saver & investor.

- Financial markets such as stock market and bond market promote greater economic efficiency by channelizing funds from savers to investors.
- Sound functioning of financial markets promote growth and prosperity in an economy

Functions of Financial Markets:

1. Financial markets facilitates price discovery for various financial instruments.
2. Financial markets provides liquidity for investors.
3. Financial markets reduces the cost of transaction.
4. Financial markets provides diversification of risk.

Classification of Financial Markets:

- Financial markets can be classified as:
1. Primary market and Secondary market (on the basis of new issue or trading of old securities),
2. Money market and Capital market (on the basis of maturity period/time).
1. **Primary Market and Secondary Market (on the basis of New Issue or Trading of Old Securities) :**
(a) **Primary Market:**
- It is the market for issuing new securities and hence, called the new issue market.
- In this market, shares, debentures and other securities are sold for the first time for collecting long-term capital.
- First time sales of equity takes place through primary market .
- As the flow of funds in capital markets is from savers to borrowers (industries), it helps directly in the capital formation.
- Money collected from this market is generally used by the corporate for the purposes of modernization, upgradation, business expansion, setting-up new business units
- Many small and medium scale businesses enter the primary market to raise money from the public to expand their businesses.
- They sell their securities to the public via the process of **Initial Public Offering [IPO].**
- Following methods can be used to raise capital in the primary market:
(i) Public Issue,
(ii) Offer For Sale,

(iii) Private Placement,

(iv) Right Issue,

(v) Electronic IPO.

(b)   Secondary Market :

- It refers to a financial market which facilitates trading of securities that have already been issued in an initial private or public offering.

- For example, if one wants to buy shares of Infosys today, he will have to buy them from secondary market.

- Thus, in secondary markets, securities that have been previously issued are resold.

- The two major secondary markets of India :

  Bombay Stock Exchange (BSE),

  National Stock Exchange (NSE).

2.   Money Market and Capital Market (on the basis of Maturity Period/Time) :

(a)   Money Market:

- According to the RBI, "The money market is the centre for dealing mainly of short character, in monetary assets; it meets the short term requirements of borrowers and provides liquidity or cash to the lenders."

- It is a place where short-term surplus investible funds at the disposal of financial and other institutions and individuals are bid by borrowers, again comprising institutions and individuals and also by the government.

  Features of Money Market :

(i) It deals in short-term borrowing and lending.

(ii) Short-term generally means a period of less than 1 year.

(iii) Through money markets, borrowers & lenders exchange short term funds to solve their liquidity needs.

(iv) It is a wholesale debt market for low-risk, highly-liquid instruments.

(v) Money market is dominated mostly by government, banks and financial institutions.

- The instruments used in the money market are near substitutes for money.

  Different Money Market Instruments:

(i) Treasury Bills,

(ii) Commercial Paper,

(iii) Money Market Mutual Fund,

(iv)   Certificates of Deposit,

(v)   Inter Corporate Deposits.

(b) Capital Market :

- It is a market for securities where corporations and governments can raise long-term funds.
- By long term, it means a market which provides funds for a period longer than a year.

   Different Capital Market Instruments :

(i)   Equity shares,

(ii)   Bonds and Debentures,

(iii)   Preference shares.

1.8 DERIVATIVES-FUTURES AND OPTIONS

Introduction :

- Derivatives are truly a financial innovation which amplifies gains as well as losses.
- Derivatives is thus, a double-edged sword.
- World's greatest investor, Warren Buffet termed derivatives as 'weapons of mass destruction'.

Definitions:

1. **Definition of Derivative as per IFRS:**
- A derivative is a financial instrument with the following three characteristics:
(i)   Its value changes in response to a change in price of, or index on, a specified underlying financial or non-financial item or other variable;
(ii)   It requires no, or comparatively little, initial investment; and
(iii)   It is to be settled at a future date.
2. **Definition of Derivative as per US GAAP:**
- A derivative instrument is a financial instrument or other contract with all three of the following characteristics:
(i)   It has one or more underlyings and one or more notional amounts or payment provisions or both. Those terms determine the amount of the settlement or settlements and in some cases, whether or not a settlement is required.

> (ii) It requires no initial net investment or an initial net investment that is smaller than would be required for other types of contracts that would be expected to have a similar response to changes in market factors.
>
> (iii) Its terms require or permit net settlement, it can readily be settled net by a means outside the contract, or it provides for delivery of an asset that puts the recipient in a position not substantially different from net settlement.

- Derivatives are thus, financial instruments that derive their value from the value of some underlying asset.
- This underlying asset could be a financial asset such as currency, stocks, government bonds, an interest bearing security or a physical commodity.
- Fluctuations in the underlying asset determines the value of the derivative. So, derivatives have no intrinsic value.
- The term "derivative" refers to a no independent value, and that the value is entirely "derived" from the value of the underlying cash asset. Hence, A derivative product is to be sharply distinguished from the underlying cash asset.
- Cash asset refers to the asset traded in the cash market on normal delivery terms.
- Examples of cash assets include the actual company shares, physical stocks of commodities, foreign currency etc.
- Financial derivatives are financial instruments that are linked to a specific financial instrument or indicator or commodity, and through which specific financial risks can be traded in financial markets in their own right...(IMF)
- Derivatives hedge the risk of owning assets that are subject to unexpected price fluctuations such as foreign currencies, stocks, crude oil, stocks .
- Derivative contract is an agreement between two parties ,wherein each does something for the other.
- Financial derivatives contracts are mostly settled by net payments of cash.
  Use of Derivatives Explained through an Example:
- A derivative contract can work well, especially between two such parties who face the opposite kind of risk.
- For example, considering the risk of currency fluctuations, exportes and importes face opposite kinds of risk.

- Exporters face losses if the rupee appreciates and importers face losses if the rupee depreciates.
- By entering into a forward contract in the dollar-rupee forward market, they supply insurance to each other and thereby, reduce risk.
- Derivatives are traded through the following:
1. Over-the-counter (OTC),
2. Exchange.
- OTC derivatives have greater proportion of derivatives .They are unregulated, and hence have greater risk for the counterparty as compared to standardized derivatives.
- On the other hand, derivatives traded on exchanges are standardized. They are regulated.

   Types of Derivative Contracts:
1. Forward Contracts,
2. Futures Contracts,
3. Options Contracts,
4. Swaps.

Participants in a Derivative Market :

1. Hedgers:
- Hedgers make use futures or options instruments to reduce or eliminate the risk associated with price of an asset.

2. Speculators:
- Speculators bet on future movements in the price of an asset.
- Using derivative contracts, they get an extra leverage.
- This use of leverage can increase both the potential gains and potential losses associated with the transaction.

3. Arbitrageurs:
- Arbitrageurs take advantage of a price discrepancy in two different markets.
- The activity 'Arbitrage' refers to risk less profits.
- For example, when futures price of an asset gets out of line with the cash price, arbitrageurs will take offsetting positions in the two markets to lock in a profit.

   Purpose of Derivative Market:

1. Price Discovery:
- In futures market, prices depend on a continuous flow of information from around the world and has a high degree of transparency.

- This kind of information and the way participants in the market absorb this information constantly changes the price of a commodity/financial security. This very process is called 'price discovery'.

2. **Risk Management :**

- This is the most important purpose of the derivatives market.
- Risk management involves identification of the desired level of risk and the actual level of risk and altering the latter to equal the former.
- Hedging is a tool used for risk management

3. **Improve Market Efficiency for the Underlying Asset :**

- One can have an exposure over a financial asset through purchase of its futures or options.
- For example, instead of buying a share of Infosys Ltd. at a market price of ₹ 2,000, one can buy an options of Infosys for around ₹ 100 and still have an exposure to this financial security.

4. **Help Reduce Market Transaction Costs :**

- As derivatives provide insurance or risk management, the cost of trading in them has to be low or investors will find it economically unsound to purchase such "insurance" for their positions.

5. **Reallocation of Risks :**

- Risks can be allocated either ,across time or among individuals with different risk-bearing capacity and preferences

   Derivatives in India:

- Derivatives trading commenced in India in June 2000 after the final approval by SEBI to this effect in May 2000.
- SEBI allowed the derivative segments of two stock exchanges, NSE and BSE, and their clearing house/corporation to commence trading and settlement in approved derivatives contracts.
- SEBI first approved trading in index futures contracts based on S&P CNX Nifty and BSE–30 (Sensex) index, which was followed by approval for trading in options based on these two indexes and options on individual securities.

(A) Futures :

- One would generally use a futures contract to hedge against risk during a particular period of time.

Definition :

> "A future is a financial contract obligating the buyer to purchase an asset and the seller to sell an asset, such as a physical commodity or a financial instrument, at a predetermined future date and price."　　**(Investopedia)**

- A future contract refers to an agreement between two parties to buy or sell a financial asset or a physical commodity at a certain time in the future at an agreed upon price.
- It is a legally binding agreement on the counter parties.
- For example, instead of buying shares of Reliance, one can buy futures of Reliance. It will give the buyer to buy a Reliance share at a fixed price after a certain period, through the payment of a certain upfront margin.
- The party that agrees to buy the underlying asset in the future(the "buyer" of the contract) is said to be "long", and the party that agrees to sell the asset in the future (the "seller" of the contract) is said to be "short".
- Futures are standardized exchange-traded contracts, traded on an exchange.
- Following terms are standardized in a futures contract:

(a)　Quantity of the underlying,

(b)　The date and month of delivery,

(c)　Place of settlement.

- Futures are traded through a counter party such as a clearing corporation, which eliminates the credit risk associated with the transaction.
- A futures contract requires both parties to put up an initial amount of cash called as the 'margin'.
- Margins is set as a percentage of the value of the futures contract, which needs to be proportionally maintained at all times during the life of the contract
- A futures contract may be off-set prior to maturity by entering into an equal and opposite transaction.

Futures are basically used for two purposes:

1.　Speculation :

- It refers to betting on the movement of a security. Here, huge money is made and lost.

2.　Hedging :

- It refers to covering of risk.

(B) Options :

- An option is a contract that gives the buyer the right, but not the obligation, to buy or sell an underlying asset at a specific price on or before a certain date.
- It is thus, a financial derivative that represents a contract sold by one party (option writer) to another party (option holder).

Types of Options :

1. Call Option,
2. Put Option.

1. Call Option :

- A call option gives the holder of the option the right to buy an asset or a financial security at a certain price within a specific period of time.
- Call option is thus, similar to having a long position on a stock.
- Buyer of a call option anticipates that the stock will increase substantially before the option expires.

Example :

- Suppose on 1st April, the stock price of Infosys Ltd. is ₹ 2,000 and the premium (for buying option of Infosys) is costing ₹ 120 for a June 2100 Call, which indicates that the expiration is the last Thursday of June and the strike price is ₹ 2,100. The total price of the contract (of say, 100 shares) is ₹ 120 × 100 = ₹ 12,000. We will ignore commissions for the time being.
- The strike price of ₹ 2,100 means that the stock price must rise above ₹ 2,100 before the call option is worth anything.
- In addition, the price of the contract is ₹ 120 per share. Hence the break-even price would be ₹ 2,220 (2,100 + 120).
- Any price rise beyond 2,220 gets profit for the buyer of the call option.
- Higher the rise, higher the profits.

2. Put Option :

- A put option gives the holder of the option the right to sell an asset or a financial security at a certain price within a specific period of time.
- Put option is thus, similar to having a short position on a stock.
- Buyer of a put option anticipates that the stock will fall substantially before the option expires.

Example :

- Suppose on 1st April, the stock price of Infosys Ltd. is ₹ 2,000 and the premium (for buying put option of Infosys) is costing ₹ 120 for a June 1,900 put which indicates that the expiration is the last Thursday of June and the strike price is ₹ 1,900.
- The total price of the contract (of say, 100 shares) is ₹ 120 × 100 = ₹ 12,000. We will ignore commissions for the time being.
- The strike price of ₹ 1,900 means that the stock price must fall below ₹ 1,900 before the put option is worth anything.
- In addition, the price of the contract is ₹ 120 per share. Hence the break-even price would be ₹ 1,780 (1,900 − 120).
- Any price fall beyond ₹ 1,780 gets profit for the buyer of the put option.
- More the fall, higher the profits.

3. American Options and European Options:

- Depending upon the right to exercise the options and the time frame available for it, options are also classified as American options and European options.
- American options can be exercised at any time between the date of purchase and the expiration date.
- European options can be exercised only on the expiry date.

  Terminologies in Options:

1. Strike Price :

- It is the pre-agreed price per share at which stock may be bought or sold under the terms of an option contract.
- Strike price is also refereed to as the "Exercise price".

2. Expiration Date :

- It refers to the last day on which an option may be exercised.
- Options expire on a specified date as per the options contract.

3. Long :

- It refers to the position created by the purchase of a futures contract or option.

4. Short :

- It refers to the position created by the sale of a futures contract or option.

Need of Options:

- Options are basically used for two purposes:

1. **Speculation :**

- It refers to betting on the movement of a security. Here, huge money is made and lost.

2. **Hedging :**

- It refers to covering of risk.
- Options are complex instruments and can be extremely risky.
- Trading in options involve risks.
- It is speculative in nature and carry substantial risk of loss.

Difference between Futures and Options:

- Both Future and Options are derivative instruments which facilitate speculation and hedging for the participants in this market.
- They both offer leverage to the related parties.
- Both are high risk and high returns instruments.
- Both are standardized contracts which have a counterparty such as CCIL, so that the credit risk for the parties to the contract is eliminated.
- However, there are certain differences between these derivative instruments.
- They are explained as follows:

Basis	Futures	Options
1. Meaning :	A future is a financial contract obligating the buyer to purchase an asset and the seller to sell an asset, such as a physical commodity or a financial instrument, at a predetermined future date and price.	An option is a contract that gives the buyer the right, but not the obligation, to buy or sell an underlying asset at a specific price on or before a certain date.
2. Compulsion to Exercise :	A futures contract will be compulsorily exercised/ settled.	Exercising an option depends upon the will of the buyer of call option or put option.
3. Pay-offs :	Linear pay-off.	Non-linear payoff.

Basis	Futures	Options
4. Transaction Date :	It is the date specified in the contract.	The transaction can be done any time on or before the expiry date specified in the contract, in case of American options.
5. Magnitude of Profit and Loss :	Potential for Profit and loss is unlimited.	Profit potential is unlimited while potential of loss for the buyer of call/put option is limited.
6. Cash Outflow :	Upfront margin is required for purchase of futures contract, which requires a large cash outflow.	In case of options, only premium amount is required to be paid which involves low cash outflow.

1.9 FOREIGN EXCHANGE MARKET

1. Introduction:

- Also referred to as FOREX market.
- Foreign exchange market is a global online network where buying and selling of currencies take place.
- By doing so, it determines the value of one currency against another currency (Exchange rate), on a daily basis.
- It has no physical location and operates 24 hours a day .
- In a foreign exchange market, buying foreign currencies with domestic currencies and selling foreign currencies for domestic currencies takes place.
- In other words, the claims to foreign moneys are bought and sold for domestic currency.
- Exporters sell foreign currencies in return for domestic currencies and importers buy foreign currencies in exchange for domestic currencies.
- In a foreign exchange market, buyers and sellers include individuals, firms, foreign exchange brokers, commercial banks and the central bank.
- Foreign exchange market is a system, not a place.

- A large number of foreign currencies are traded, converted and exchanged in the FOREX market.
- Forex market is the largest and most liquid financial market in the world with an estimated turnover of $7 trillion a day.
- In India, the foreign exchange market is controlled by Reserve Bank of India (RBI) through the act called as Foreign Exchange Management Act, 1999 (FEMA).

2. **Structure of FOREX Market:**

- In a foreign exchange market, central banks are at the apex, followed by brokers, and then by the Commercial banks.
- The last leg constitutes entities who actually use the currency for their requirements , such as exporters and importers, immigrants, investors, tourists.
- These constitutes the major players in a FOREX market, as shown in the figure below:

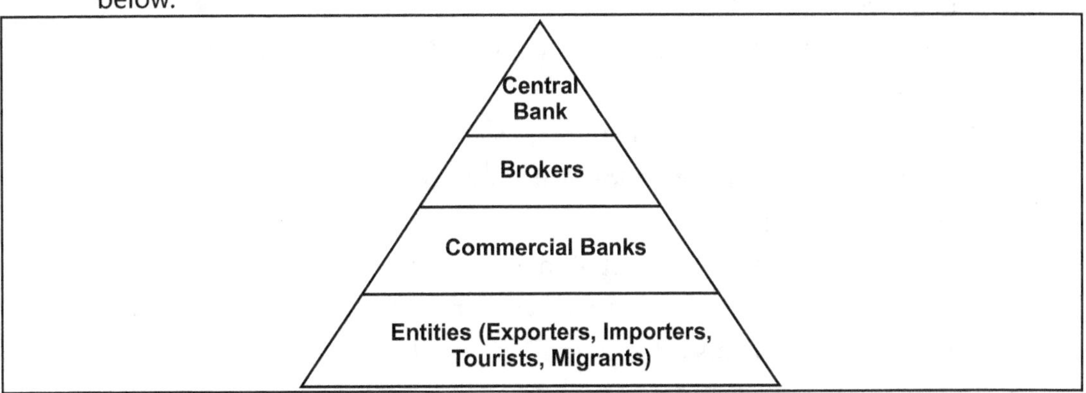

Fig. 1.3 : Structure of Forex Market

(a) **Central Bank :**

- Central bank of a country is the apex body in the foreign exchange market, which acts as custodian of foreign exchange of the country.
- The central bank is the regulator and controller of the foreign exchange market , and ensures that this market works in an orderly fashion.
- At times, Central bank even makes direct intervention in the FOREX market, to prevent the aggressive fluctuations in the currency.

(b) **Brokers :**

- Foreign exchange brokers act as a link between the central bank and the commercial banks , as well as between the actual buyers and commercial banks.
- They even provide market information.

- Brokers do not themselves buy or sell the foreign currency, but rather strike a deal between the buyer and the seller on a commission basis.

(c) Commercial Banks :

- Commercial banks dealing in foreign exchange play an important role of "market makers".
- They quote the foreign exchange rates for buying and selling of the foreign currencies on a daily basis.
- Additionally, they function as clearing houses, wherein they buy the currencies from the brokers and sell it to the buyers.

(d) Actual Users (Exporters, Importers, Tourists) :

- At the bottom of a pyramid are the actual buyers and sellers of the foreign currencies which includes entities such as exporters, importers, tourist, investors, and immigrants.
- For instance, Importers need foreign currency to buy goods from their overseas suppliers.

3. Functions of Foreign Exchange Market:

Foreign exchange market performs the following functions:

(a) Transfer Function :

- This is the basic and the most visible function of foreign exchange market. The transfer of funds (foreign currency) from one country to another for the settlement of payments is facilitated.
- In other words, conversion of one currency to another takes place which transfers the purchasing power from one country to another.
- Transfer function is performed through credit instruments like bills of foreign exchange, bank drafts and telephonic transfers.
- For example, If Importer in India import goods from USA ,then the payment has to be made in US currency (dollars).The exporter , for this purpose, converts rupee to the dollar and this conversion will be facilitated by FOREX.

(b) Credit Function :

- FOREX market provides credit for foreign trade, through instruments such as bills of exchange, generally with maturity period of three months.
- With this credit, importer can make foreign purchases.
- For example, an Indian company can import machinery from the USA, and pay for this purchase by issuing a bill of exchange in the foreign exchange market.

(c) Hedging Function :

- Hedging function helps the parties in foreign exchange transaction to mitigate the fear of the fluctuations in the exchange rates.

- Exporters and importers enter into an agreement to sell and buy goods on some future date at the current prices and exchange rate.

- For example, if an importer in India purchases a machinery for USD 1,000 and has to make payment in dollars after 3 months, he can lock in USD 1,000 at current exchange rate, so that he does not incur any loss, even if the value of US dollar increases within 3 months.

4. Types of Foreign Exchange Markets :

- Depending on the nature of transactions, foreign exchange market is classified into two broad categories- Spot market and Forward market.

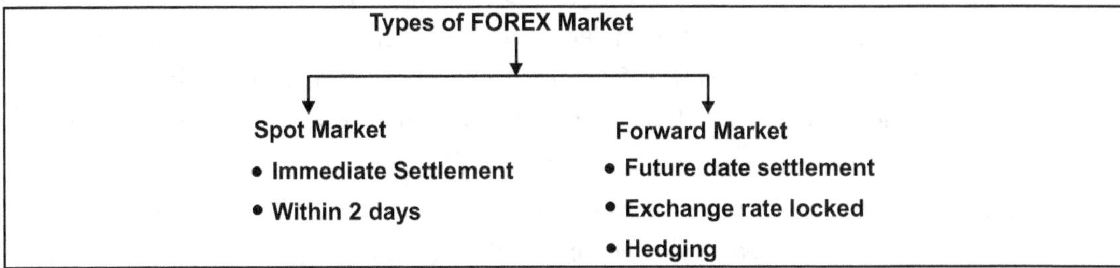

Fig. 1.4 : Types of Foreign Exchange Market

(a) Spot Market :

- Spot market refers to immediate delivery market , wherein receipts and payments are made immediately.

- The sale and purchase transactions of currency are settled within two days of the deal .

- In spot market, the spot sale and purchase of foreign exchange takes place and the rate at which the transaction is settled is called a Spot Exchange Rate, which in turn is the prevailing exchange rate in the market.

- Spot market is of daily nature and deals only in spot transactions of foreign exchange , and not in future transactions

(b) Forward Market :

- Forward market refers to the market in which sale and purchase of foreign currency is settled at some specified date in future, at an exchange rate which is agreed upon today. Such a transaction is called as 'Forward Transaction' and the exchange rate agreed upon is known as the 'Forward Rate'.

- Forward transaction is used for hedging purposes, which can be used to mitigate currency fluctuation issue for the parties involved in a foreign exchange transaction.

1.10 CRYPTO-CURRENCY MARKET

1. **Concept of Crypto-currency :**

- Crypto currency is a digital currency or virtual currency designed to function as a medium of exchange.
- The technology of cryptography is used to secure the transactions, to control the creation of additional units, and to verify the transfer of assets.
- Several crypto-currencies such as Bitcoin, Ethereum, Primecoin exist worldwide.
- Cryptography technology used in crypto-currency makes it nearly impossible to counterfeit or double-spend. In fact, the name Cryptocurrency is derived from the word "Crypto", which refers to the various encryption algorithms and cryptographic techniques that safeguard the ledger entries internal to the system such as public-private key pairs, and hashing functions.
- Crypto currencies can be classified as a sub-set of digital currencies, and of alternative currencies and virtual currencies.
- Cryptocurrencies are decentralized and are produced by the entire cryptocurrency system collectively, at a rate which is defined when the system is created and which is publicly known.
- Being decentralized, Crypto-currency is not issued by any central bank or such authority like RBI (Reserve Bank of India). Hence, it is safe from government interference or manipulation, and exist outside the control of governments and central banks. Moreover, companies or governments cannot produce new units.
- Bitcoin, a peer-to-peer online virtual currency created in 2009, was the first decentralized crypto currency.
- It was based on blockchain, or a large set of data that represents every Bitcoin transaction.
- All purchases are recorded in the block chain, confirming an owner's possession of Bitcoins.
- The users simply download the wallet program and use it to purchase or receive Bitcoins.

Advantages :

- Cryptocurrencies have been appreciated throughout the world for following reasons:

(a) Easy transferability with minimal processing fees.

(b) Portability.

(c) Decentralization, thereby immune to decisions of institutions like Central bank or Government.

(d) Divisibility.

(e) Anonymity of users, and privacy.

(f) Resistance to inflation.

(g) Security.

Limitations :

- However, Crypto-currencies face some apprehensions, as below:

(a) Their use for illegal activities such as money laundering and tax evasion.

(b) Exchange rate volatility.

(c) Vulnerabilities of the infrastructure underlying them.

- Though Governments and Central banks have been skeptical about crypto-currencies, these entities are exploring the underlying Blockchain technology in crypto-currencies for financial transactions in terms of speed , security and other benefits.

2. **Bitcoin :**

- In centralized banking and economic systems , Central banks or governments control the supply of currency by printing units of fiat money or demanding additions to digital banking ledgers.

- However, Bitcoin is the first decentralized cryptocurrency, a peer-to-peer online virtual currency created in 2009.

- The decentralized control is related to the use of bitcoin's blockchain transaction database in the role of a distributed ledger.

- There exist no physical Bitcoins, only balances are kept on a public ledger in the cloud, which are verified by a huge amount of computing power.

- Bitcoin is deregulated and maintains the anonymity of its holders.

- Bitcoins are created by the group or individual allegedly named Satoshi Nakamoto.

- Nakamoto created a sophisticated formula , which when solved using computer processing power, creates a block of data that contains Bitcoins.
- The underlying technique behind Bitcoin is referred to as Blockchain, or a large set of data that represents every Bitcoin transaction.
- All purchases are recorded in the block chain, confirming an owner's possession of Bitcoins.
- The users simply download the wallet program and use it to purchase or receive Bitcoins.
- Blockchain technology is used to keep an online ledger of all the transactions that have ever been conducted, hence providing a data structure for this ledger.
- It is very safe and is shared and agreed upon by the entire network of individual node, or computer maintaining a copy of the ledger.
- Every new block generated must be verified by each node before being confirmed, making it almost impossible to forge transaction histories.
- Many experts perceive blockchain technology as having serious potential use in area of finance, law, online voting and crowd funding.
- Though Governments and Central banks have been skeptical about Bitcoins, they are exploring the underlying Blockchain technology for financial transactions.
- In fact, RBI has concluded in its white paper, that blockchain is indeed a disruptive technology that can potentially revolutionise the financial industry.
- In India, Yes Bank, ICICI and Axis Bank have already started providing financial services using block chain technology to some of their clients.

3. **Market :**
- There are several ways to purchase and sell Crypto-currencies, ordinarily accomplished through a currency exchange.
- For example, in case of Bitcoins, MtGox.com is the oldest and most popular exchange site for USD. MtGox.com lists prices for buyers and sellers of Bitcoins. It then matches up two interested exchangers and arranges the transaction.
- Users can also exchange various gift cards to trade for Bitcoins instead of some regulated currencies such as USD, or INR.
- Users can also make a direct exchange through Bitcoin miners.

1.11 COMMODITY MARKET

1. **Basics :**

- Commodity market is a place where in a wide range of products such as precious metals, energy, crude oil, coffee, pulses, spices etc. are traded.
- Commodity market is sort of a financial market that deals with raw materials ,or the primary economic sector.
- Commodity markets enable investors to trade in several commodities, and these commodities are divided into soft commodities(such as cocoa or spices) and hard commodities (such as oil or gold).
- Through commodity markets, investors can invest in the price of different commodities in the form of CFDs (Contract For Difference).
- The investors simply invest in the price of a specific commodity without having to actually own it.
- Commodity trading can be done online.
- Trading in commodity markets can include physical trading and derivatives trading using spot prices, forwards, futures, and other complex derivative mechanisms.
- Financial derivatives are financial instruments that are linked to a specific financial instrument or indicator or commodity, and through which specific financial risks can be traded in financial markets in their own right.
- In other words, derivatives derive their price from the underlying asset (here, the underlying asset is the commodity being traded).
- Most of the trading in commodities happens through futures contracts.
- Futures are secured by physical assets.
- A futures contract refers to an agreement between the buyer and the seller, wherein the buyer promises to pay the agreed-upon sum at the moment of the transaction when the seller delivers the commodity at a pre-decided date in the future.
- For example, a farmer can buy wheat futures to fix a price at which he would sell a certain amount of wheat at a specified date in future.
- Even trader can buy or sell wheat futures for delivery on a future date at a price decided today.

- Also, one can trade or invest in commodities through some exchange-traded funds(ETF's) that specialize in certain commodities. For example, Gold ETF.
- Organized commodity trading started in 1848 with the establishment of the Chicago Board of Trade (CBOT).
- In India, organized trading in commodities initiated the constitution of the Bombay Cotton Trade Association in the year 1875.
- Forward Markets Commission (FMC), a division of the Ministry of Consumer Affairs, Food and Public Distribution is the regulator for Commodity futures in India.
- In 2015, FMC was merged with SEBI.

2. **Commodity Exchanges in India :**

- India produces a large number of commodities , and also has a long history of trading in commodities and related derivatives.
- However, commodity futures markets are largely underdeveloped due to extensive government intervention in the agriculture sector.
- In India, three major commodity exchanges are in operation, i.e.,

(a) National Commodity & Derivative Exchange (NCDEX),

(b) Multi Commodity Exchange (MCX),

(c) National Multi Commodity Exchange of India (NMCE).

- MCX is the largest commodity futures exchange in India, with a market share of around 70%.
- Several commodities of varied types can be traded in commodity markets, some of which are given below:

(a) Industrial Metals such as Copper, Aluminium, Cobalt , Nickel, Lead, Tin, Zinc etc.

(b) Precious metals such as Gold, Silver, Platinum.

(c) Energy which includes Crude Oil, Brent Crude Oil, Natural Gas, Ethanol etc.

(d) Spices such as Cardamom, Turmeric, Pepper, Jeera, Red Chilli.

(e) Plantations such as Cashew, Coffee, Rubber.

(f) Cereals such as Potato, Maize, Guar seed.

(g) Several other Agricultural commodities.

(h) Oil & Oilseeds and Cotton.

3. Advantages of Commodity Futures Market:

(a) Price Discovery :
- On the basis of information such as Government policy, amount of production of the commodity, climate, demand and supply, buyers and sellers conduct trading at futures exchanges.
- This results into continuous price discovery mechanism and assessment of fair value of a particular commodity.

(b) Hedging :
- Price risk can be managed by business by taking an equal but opposite position in the futures market.
- With such a position, businesses can protect themselves from adverse price change.
- For example, if a bread manufacturer wants to protect himself from possibly a huge rise in the price of wheat, he can buy Wheat futures.

(c) Portfolio Diversification :
- Commodity returns usually have low or negative correlations with the returns of other major asset classes such as stocks and bonds.
- When price of stocks fall, price of commodities generally rise.
- Hence, commodities can act as an excellent tool for portfolio diversification

(d) Protection against Inflation :
- Commodities such as gold and other precious metals find value during rising inflation.
- Real value of Financial assets such as stocks and bonds erodes during high inflation.
- Commodities, nevertheless, maintain their value and price even during periods of high inflation.

(e) Import- Export Competitiveness :
- Exporters and importers can hedge their price risk and improve their competitiveness by making use of futures market.
- Many traders which are involved in physical trade internationally intend to buy forwards.
- The existence of futures market allows the exporters to hedge their future purchase by temporarily substituting for actual purchase till the time is suitable for them to buy in physical market.

(f)   Standardization and Improved Product Quality :

- The existence of warehouses for facilitating delivery, alongwith benefits such as grading facilities and quality certification leads to up gradation and enhancement the quality of the commodity to grade that is acceptable by the exchange.
- This mechanism guarantees uniform standardization of commodity trade which can become the norm for physical trade.

1.12 BOND MARKETS

1.   Concept of a Bond Market :

- Also referred to as debt market or credit market.
- Bond markets is a financial marketplace where investors can trade in debt securities issued by Government and corporate.
- Bonds make fixed periodic payments and additionally repay the principal amount on maturity.
- Moreover, investors can profit if they resell the bonds at a higher price in the secondary market.
- The bond market is broadly classified into primary market and the secondary market.
- In the primary market, transactions takes place directly between the bond issuers and the bond buyers. In this way, the primary market leads to the creation of new debt securities.
- In the secondary market, securities already sold in the primary market are traded.
- Investors can purchase bonds from a broker who acts as an intermediary between the buying and selling parties.
- The secondary market issues may be packaged in the form of pension funds, mutual funds, and life insurance polices among many other product structures.
- The bond market is an over-the-counter market, meaning that there is no trading floor or other centralized location such as NSE.
- In the Treasury bond market, interdealer brokers facilitate trades between bond dealers, and disseminate the prices at which trades take place. Inter-dealer trades involve huge price deals in large block.

- The bond markets are influenced by expectations regarding the change in economic growth and inflation.
- When investors expect a high rate of inflation, they will pay less for bonds, and vice-versa.
- Bond prices and bond yields are inversely related. When bond prices fall, yields rise, and vice versa.
- Yield measures the value of a bond to an investor, or the returns investors receive from a bond.

  Example :

- Suppose a company issues a 10-year bond with a 8% coupon at a price of 100 to yield 8%. And due to some negative news, the bond's price falls to 98, its yield will be boosted to 8.2%.(8/98*100).
- Several Bond Indices exist such as Barclays Capital Aggregate Bond Index, Citigroup U.S., Broad Investment-Grade Bond Index, which manage and measure bond portfolio performance.

2. **Types of Bonds :**

(a) **Government Bonds :**

- Referred to as Treasury bond markets.
- Governments typically issue bonds in order to raise capital for infrastructure projects such as roads, power, telecom etc.
- Government bonds generally pay the face value listed on the bond certificate on the agreed maturity date, as well as periodic interest payments.
- The additional characteristic of safety makes government bonds attractive to conservative investors.

(b) **Corporate Bonds :**

- Publicly listed corporates issue bonds when they need to finance business expansion projects or maintain current operations, expanding product lines, or opening up new manufacturing facilities.
- Corporate bonds are long-term debt instruments having a maturity of more than one year.

(c) **Municipal Bonds :**

- Municipal bonds are locally issued bonds.
- They are issued by local government or their agencies, who seek to raise funds for various projects.

Questions For Discussion

1. Explain in detail, the concept of Financial System. State its role in Economic development of the country.
2. Explain the structure of financial system in detail.
3. Explain an overview of Indian financial system
4. What are Financial markets ? Explain its classification, and functions.
5. What are the characteristics of financial instruments?
6. What is a bank? Explain the various functions of banks.
7. What are derivatives? Explain Futures and Options in detail.
8. Explain Foreign exchange markets with regards to its structure, functions and types.
9. Write a detailed note on Crypto-currency markets.
10. Write a detailed note on Bond markets.
11. Explain Commodity markets. List the advantages of Commodities futures market.
12. **Write short notes on :**

(A) Financial Institutions. (B) Financial Markets.
(C) Financial Instruments. (D) Financial Services.
(E) Money market. (F) Capital market.
(G) Primary market. (H) Secondary market.
(I) Banking Institutions and Non-bank institutions.
(J) Contribution of banks in Economic development.
(K) Agency functions of bank. (L) Futures.
(M) Options. (N) Call option.
(O) Put option. (P) Participants in Derivative market.
(Q) Purpose of Derivative market. (R) Commodity exchanges in India.
(S) Bitcoin. (T) Spot market.
(U) Forward market.

Money Market

Contents ...

Learning Objectives...

After studying this chapter, the student should understand:

- Concept of Money Market.
- Structure and Components of Money Market.
- Unorganised and Organised Money market.
- Money Market Instruments-Treasury bills, CD, CP, CBLO, MMMF's, Call money market.
- Participants/Players in the Indian Money Market.
- Role of central bank in money market.
- Reforms undertaken in Indian Money Market.

2.1 INTRODUCTION TO MONEY MARKET

- The money market is a market for short-term financial securities which are close substitutes of money.
- In other words, Money market is a sub-section of the financial market which trades in short term financial securities.
- The most important feature of a money market instrument is liquidity, wherein financial securities can be turned into money quickly .

- Money market is different from capital markets, in which transaction of long-term financial securities takes place.

Definitions of Money Market :

1. **Geoffrey :**

   "Money market is the collective name given to the various firms and institutions that deal in the various grades of the near money."

2. **Prof. Crowther :**

   "Money Market is a collective name given to the various firms and institutions that deal in various grades of money."

3. **As per Madden and Naddler :**

   "Money Market is a mechanism through which short term funds are loaned and financial transactions of a particular country or of the world are cleared."

4. **Reserve Bank of India(RBI) :**

   "Money Market is the centre for dealings mainly for short term character, in monetary assets. It makes the short term requirements of borrowers and provides liquidity or cash to the lenders."

- It deals in short-term borrowing and lending.
- Short-term generally means a period of less than 1 year. Thus, money market instruments have a maturity period ranging from 1 day to 1 year.
- Through money markets, borrowers & lenders exchange short term funds to solve their liquidity needs.
- It is a wholesale debt market for low-risk, highly-liquid instruments.
- Unlike the stock exchange, the money market does not have a geographical location.
- Most transactions happen in the virtual world with institutions that can be spread out over the entire country.
- An important feature of the money market is honor of commitment and creditworthiness.
- The nature of money market transactions is such that they are large in amount and high in volume.
- Money market is dominated mostly by government, banks and financial institutions.
- The instruments used in the money market are near substitutes for money.

- RBI regulates the money market in India.

Money Market Instruments :

- Different money market instruments are as follows:

1. Call and notice money.
2. Treasury bills.
3. Commercial paper.
4. Money Market Mutual Fund.
5. Certificates of deposit.
6. Inter corporate deposits.

- These money market instruments ,generally differ on the basis of:

1. Maturity,
2. Purpose,
3. Participants,
4. Amounts.

Importance of Money Market :

1. Provides finance to trade and industry.
2. Provides investors with a short-term avenue to invest funds.
3. Commercial banks can use their excess reserves in profitable investment opportunities.
4. Commercial banks can, in case of emergency, borrow from money markets to meet their requirements.
5. Highly liquid instruments are available in money market.
6. Money markets help a Central Bank in transmission of its monetary policy and to regulate the levels of liquidity in the economy.
7. Money market provides an important source of finance to government. Government raises finance from money market via issuing treasury bills.
8. Money markets promote economic growth, as they make funds available to various units in the economy such as agriculture, small scale industries, and others.
9. Encourages savings and investments.
10. Helps corporate with short-term deficits to manage with their working capital requirements.

2.2 STRUCTURE AND COMPONENTS OF MONEY MARKET

- The Indian money market is broadly divided into two different parts, i.e., the unorganised and organised segments.
- These two segments have a lot of differences.
- The organised sector of the Indian money market is a fairly integrated one, whereas the unorganised segment of the Indian money market is not an integrated sector.
- The unorganised money market can also be known as an unauthorized money market
- Thus, there are two main sources of supply of short-term funds in the Indian money market, i.e.,
1. Unorganised indigenous sector, and
2. Organised formal sector.
- The unorganised sector comprises numerous indigenous bankers and village money lenders.
- The organised sector includes the nationalised and private sector commercial banks, the foreign banks, co-operative banks and the Reserve Bank of India (RBI).
- **Chart below shows the Structure of Indian Money Market :**

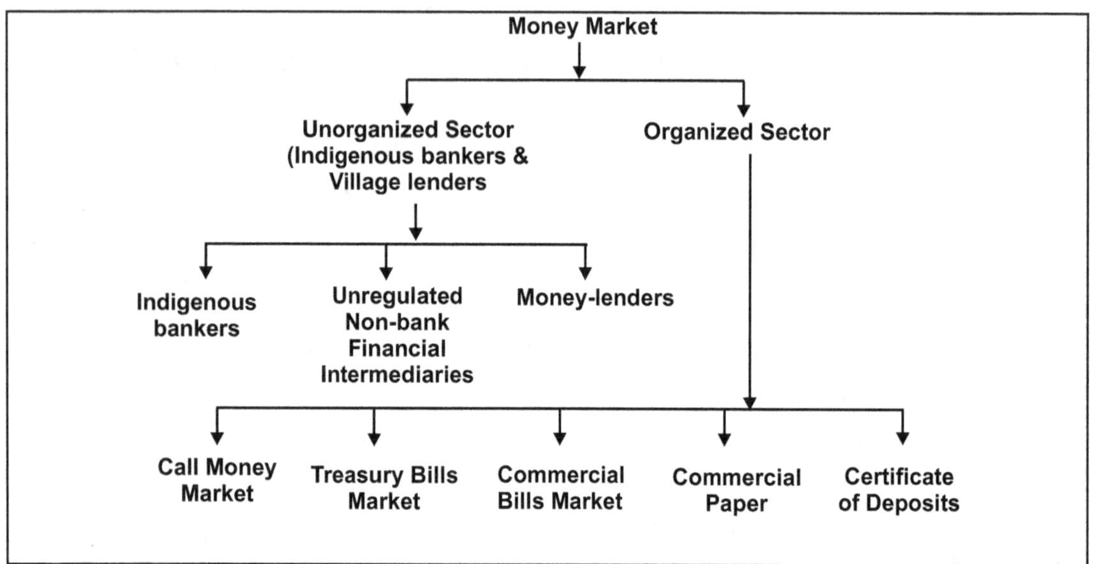

Fig. 2.1 : Structure of Indian Money Market

1. **Unorganised Sector of Indian Money Market (Unorganised Indigenous Sector) :**

- The activities of the Unorganised sector of the money market are not controlled and co-ordinated by the Reserve Bank of India.
- Unorganised segment of the Indian money market is composed of unregulated non-bank financial intermediaries, indigenous bankers and money lenders.
- These entities exist in the small towns as well as in big cities, though their lending activities are mostly restricted to small towns and villages.
- Weaker sections of the society normally borrow from this unorganised sector.
- Thus, the major clientele of these entities in the unorganised sector includes farmers, artisans, small traders and small scale producers who do not have access to modern banks and financial institutions.
- The following are a few constituents of unorganised money market in India :

(a)   Indigenous Bankers :

- Indigenous bankers refer to individuals and private firms engaged in the business of receiving deposits and giving loans. Thus, they act like a mini bank.
- Their activities have no regulation.
- During the ancient and medieval periods, these indigenous bankers were very active. However, with the growth of modern banking and the growth of commercial banks and co-operative banks, the business of the indigenous bankers received a setback.
- Still, a few thousands of indigenous bankers are operating in the western and southern parts of the country and engaging themselves in the traditional banking business.
- The lending operations of Indigenous bankers remain mostly unregulated and unsupervised. They charge high rate of interest .
- Indigenous bankers are further divided into four main sub-groups, depending upon their area of operation, viz.,

(i)   Gujarati Shroffs (mostly operating in Mumbai, Kolkata and in industrial and trading cities of Gujarat),

(ii)   Multani-or Shikarpuri Shroffs (operating mainly in Mumbai and Chennai),

(iii) Chettiars (operating in the South), and

(iv)   Marwari, Kayast (operating in Mumbai, Kolkata, tea gardens of Assam and also in different other parts of North-East India.

(b)   Unregulated Non-Bank Financial Intermediaries:
- These include loan or finance companies, chit funds and 'nidhis'.
- A good number of finance companies in India are engaged in collecting substantial amount of funds in the form of deposits, borrowings and other receipts.
- These NBFC's normally give loans to wholesale traders, retailers, artisans, and different self-employed persons.
- The interest rate is very high, ranging from 36 to 48 per cent p.a.
- Various types of chit funds operate in India, mainly in Tamil Nadu and Kerala.
- 'Nidhis' are a kind of mutual benefit funds restricted to its members operating majorly in South India.

(c)   Moneylenders :
- Moneylenders provide loans to small borrowers such as small and marginal farmers, agricultural labourers, artisans, factory workers, small traders etc.
- They provide loans at very high rates of interest.
- Moreover, they have also been found to adopt various malpractices for manipulating loan records of poor borrowers.
- There are both, Professional moneylenders (sole activity of Money lending) , as well as, Non-professional moneylenders in the market.
- The activity area of moneylenders are quite localised.
- Their operational methods are also not uniform.
- As the activity of moneylenders is totally unregulated and unsupervised ,it leads to exploitation of the poor sections of society.

2.   Organised Sector of Indian Money Market (Organised Formal Sector) :
- As the name suggests, the 'Organised' segment of Indian money market is quite integrated and well organised .
- The organised segments of the Indian money market is composed of the following entities:
- (a)   Reserve Bank of India (RBI),
- (b)   Commercial banks including SBI(State bank of India),
- (c)   Co-operative banks,
- (d)   Foreign banks,
- (e)   Financial institutes,
- (f)   Discount and Finance House of India (DFHI).

- The leading centres of the organised sectors of the Indian money market are Mumbai, Kolkata, Chennai, Delhi, Bangalore and Ahmedabad.

Constituents of Organised Sector of Indian Money Market :

- The main constituents of the Organised sector of Indian money market are given below:

(a) Call Money Market :

- Also known as the 'Inter-bank call money market'.
- "Call Money Market" refers to the money that is lent for one day in money market.
- In other words, money is lent and borrowed for one day.
- This extremely liquid call /notice money market is the an indicator of the day to day interest rates.
- A fall in call money indicates a rise in the liquidity and vice versa
- The call money market is an important part of the Indian Money Market, wherein the day-to-day surplus funds (usually of banks) are traded.
- Banks borrow in call markets in case of their temporary mismatches in funds and also to meet the CRR & SLR requirements stipulated by the Central bank. Hence, call money market is also known as 'Inter-bank market' or 'Inter bank loan market'.

    Participants in Call Market:

- (i)   RBI (Central bank),
- (ii) Banks,
- (iii) Financial institutions,
- (iv) Primary dealers,
- (v)   Specialized institutes like the LIC, UTI, DFHI and the NABARD.

(b) Treasury Bills Market :

- Treasury bills are an instrument for sale and purchase of short-term government securities.
- Treasury bills are promissory notes or financial bills issued by the RBI on behalf of the Government of India.
- Treasury bills (T-bills) offer short-term investment opportunities of up to one year.
- They are useful in managing short-term liquidity.
- Default risk is absent in case of T-bills as these are issued by the Government. As a result, they have become very popular.

- Banks are the major buyers of T-bills as they are eligible for inclusion in SLR.
- Government of India issues the following three types of treasury bills through auctions :

(i) 91-day T-bills,

(ii) 182-day T-bills,

(iii) 364-day T-bills.

Amount:

- Treasury bills are available for a minimum amount of ₹25,000 and in multiples of ₹ 25,000.
- Treasury bills are issued at a discount and are redeemed at face value/par value..
- For example, a Treasury bill of face value ₹ 100 might be issued at ₹ 97 (a discount of ₹ 3. However, on maturity of this T-bill, the investor will receive ₹100 (face value/par value). 3 ₹ is thus an interest for the investor.

(c) Commercial Bill Market:

- The Commercial bill market is meant to deal with trade bills or the commercial bills.
- Commercial bill is normally drawn by one merchant firm on the other and they arise out of commercial transactions.
- The purpose for issuing a commercial bill is to reimburse the seller as and when the buyer delays payment. However, the commercial bill market has not developed much in India, due to wide use of cash credit system in bank lending .

(d) Commercial Paper (CP) Market:

- Commercial papers are issued by corporations with a high credit rating.
- A listed company having working capital not less than ₹ 5 crore can issue CP.
- They are issued for meeting short-term requirements such as payroll expenses, operating expenses, and current assets.
- For the corporate, commercial papers serve as an alternative to bank borrowing.
- Infact, corporate can borrow at better interest rates through the Commercial papers
- CPs are freely transferable by endorsement and delivery.

Maturity:

- Typically 1 to 270 days.

(e) Certificate of Deposits (CD's) Market:

- A CD is a negotiable money market instrument issued by a commercial bank in dematerialized form for a specified period of time at a market determined discount rate.
- The face value is payable on maturity by the issuing bank.
- CD's are issued by banks and financial institutions to individuals, corporations, trusts, funds and associations.
- A Certificate of Deposit is a time deposit product commonly offered to consumers by banks.
- Sometimes, a bank may not have enough funds to provide a loan so it takes the help of CDs to bridge this shortfall.
- They are issued at a discount rate freely determined by the issuer and the market/investors.

Maturity :

- Maturity period of CD's ranges from 7 days to 1 year.
- Being negotiable instrument, CDs are freely transferable by endorsement and delivery.

Participants :

(i) Banks and Financial institutions (issuers).

(ii) Individuals, corporations, NRI's (Investors).

Amount :

- Banks have the freedom to issue CDs depending on their funding requirements.
- CD's are issued in multiples of ₹ 1 lakh thereafter.

(f) Money Market Mutual Fund :

- Money market mutual fund "means a scheme of a mutual fund which has been set up with the objective of investing exclusively in money market instruments."

– (SEBI)

- It is a mutual fund that is required by law to invest in low-risk securities.
- The objective of Money Market Mutual Fund is to provide investors with highest possible current income, along with preservation of capital and liquidity from investing in a diversified portfolio of short term money market securities.
- A money market mutual fund offers the easiest way for individuals to gain access to the money market.

- Money market mutual funds typically invest in money market instruments such as Certificates of deposit, Commercial paper of companies, Government securities (T-bills), or Securities which are having a high liquidity and a low risk.

(g) CBLO (Collateralized Borrowing and Lending Obligation) Market :

- CBLO is a money market instrument that represents an obligation between a borrower and a lender. This obligation is with regards to the terms and conditions of a loan.
- The financial entities who are restricted from participating in the interbank call money market in India, use CBLO to participate in the short-term money markets.
- In India, Collateralized Borrowing and Lending Obligations (CBLOs) is a money market segment, operated by the Clearing Corporation of India Ltd. (CCIL).
- In terms of functioning and objectives, the CBLO market is quite similar to the call money market.
- In the CBLO market, financial entities can access short-term loans. However, this loan is availed by providing prescribed securities as collateral, which is in contrast to the call money market.
- Several financial entities such as Banks (nationalized, private, foreign and co-operative banks), NBFC, Insurance Companies, Mutual Funds, Pension funds, Primary Dealers, Corporate are eligible for membership to CBLO.

Difference between Organised Sector and Unorganised Sector of Indian Money Market :

Basis	Organised sector	Unorganised sector
1. Regulation :	Strictly Regulated(RBI).	Not regulated.
2. Supervision :	Highly supervised.	Non-supervised.
3. Uniformity :	Present.	No uniformity between different organisations.
4. Malpractices :	Rare.	Common.

2.3 PARTICIPANTS/PLAYERS IN THE INDIAN MONEY MARKET

- Money markets attract players who wish to park their surplus for short-term in the money market(thereby acting as lenders), or those who wish to borrow funds for short-term(thereby acting as borrowers). As a result, money market has a large number of participants.

- These participants are either borrowers in the money market, or lenders in the money market, or both.

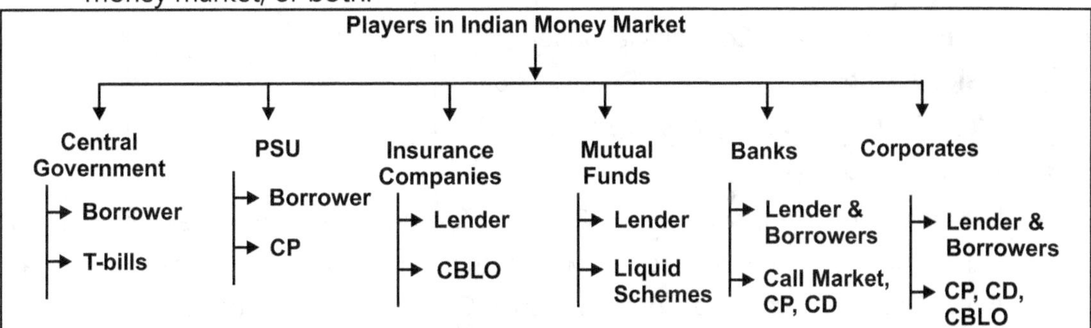

Fig. 2.2 : Participants /Players in the Indian Money Market

- Some major participants in money market are described below:

1. Central Government :

- Central Government is basically, a borrower in the money market.
- The Government issues Treasury Bills (T-Bills), through the country's central bank, RBI.
- The T-Bills instruments carry zero risk. This is because they are issued by the Government, through RBI.
- Due to this very risk free nature of T-bills, they are often purchased by banks, corporate and many such institutions ,thus providing short-term finance to the Government .
- T-bills are issued with the following tenures:

(a) 91 days (3 months),

(b) 182 days (6 months), and

(c) 364 days (1 year).

Snapshot:

Category : Borrower
Instruments Used : T-bills
Risk : Risk-free (Zero risk)
Maturity Period : 3 months to 1 year

2. Public Sector Undertakings (PSU):

- PSUs are basically borrowers in the money market.
- Since many government-owned companies are listed on stock exchanges, they can issue commercial paper.
- The money raised through Commercial papers provide working capital finance to PSU.

Snapshot :

> **Category :** Borrower
>
> **Instruments Used :** Commercial papers
>
> **Risk :** Very low
>
> **Maturity Period :** 3 months to 1 year

3. **Insurance Companies :**

- Life insurance companies and General life insurance companies are basically lenders in the money market. However, their investments in money market are limited, as they invest most of their cash in Capital market instruments.
- They invest in money markets, basically through CBLO (Collateralized Borrowing and Lending Obligations)

Snapshot :

> **Category :** Lender
>
> **Instruments used :** CBLO
>
> **Risk :** Low
>
> **Maturity Period :** 1 day to 1 year

4. **Mutual Funds :**

- Mutual funds are basically lenders in the money market.
- Mutual funds offer varieties of schemes, according to different investment objectives of their clients.
- Schemes such as Money Market Mutual Fund Schemes or Liquid Schemes invest in money market instruments.
- These Liquid schemes offer highest liquidity to the investors of mutual fund schemes.
- Withdrawal can be made by way of a day's notice as well.

Snapshot :

> **Category :** Lender.
>
> **Instruments used :** Liquid mutual fund schemes.
>
> **Risk :** Low.
>
> **Maturity Period :** 1 day to 1 year.

5. **Banks :**

- Scheduled commercial banks act as borrowers as well as lenders in the money market.

- They borrow and lend in call money market, short-notice market, repo and reverse repo market.
- They even buy the commercial papers issued by corporate and listed public sector units.
- As regards to borrowing, they borrow through issue of Certificate of Deposits to the corporate.

  Snapshot :

  > **Category :** Lender and Borrower
  >
  > **Instruments used :** Call market, Commercial papers, Certificate of deposits
  >
  > **Risk :** Low
  >
  > **Maturity Period :** 1 day to 1 year

6. **Corporates :**

- Corporates act as borrowers as well as lenders in the money market.
- They borrow via issue of commercial papers.
- These papers are issued by listed companies after obtaining the necessary credit rating for these instruments.
- Moreover, Corporates also lend in the CBLO market their temporary surplus, when the interest rate rules very high in the market.
- They also act as lenders when they buy the Certificate of Deposit issued by the banks.
- In addition, they are the lenders when they make purchase of Treasury bills.

  Snapshot :

  > **Category :** Lender and Borrower
  >
  > **Instruments Used :** Commercial papers, Certificate of deposits, T-bills, CBLO
  >
  > **Risk :** Low
  >
  > **Maturity Period :** 1 day to 1 year

- Apart from these big players, small players like Non-banking Finance companies (NBFC's), Primary dealers (PD), Provident funds and Pension funds invest and borrow in the money market, mainly through CBLO instruments.

2.4 MONEY MARKET INSTRUMENTS-TREASURY BILLS, CD, CP, CBLO, MMMF'S, CALL MONEY MARKET

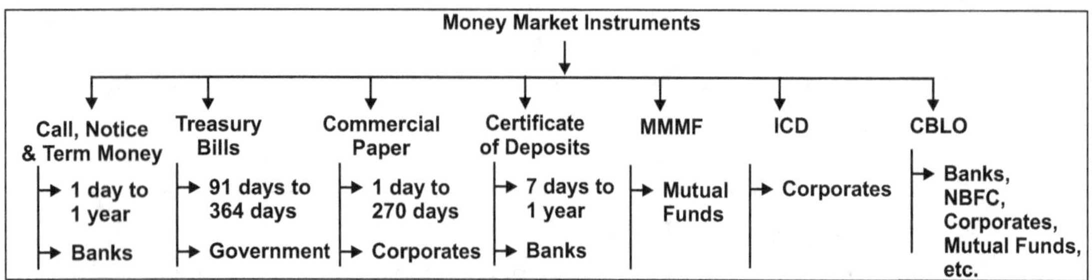

Fig. 2.3 : Money Market Instruments

1. **Call, Notice and Term Money :**

- "Call Money" refers to the money that is lent for one day in money market.

- For "Notice Money" ,the maturity ranges from 1 day to 14 days.

- This extremely liquid call /notice money market is an indicator of the day to day interest rates.

- A fall in call money indicates a rise in the liquidity and vice versa

- The rate at which money is made available is called as a Call rate. This rate is determined by the market forces such as the demand for and supply of money.

- The call money market is an important part of the Indian Money Market, wherein the day-to-day surplus funds (usually of banks) are traded.

- Banks borrow in call markets in case of their temporary mis-matches in funds and also to meet the CRR & SLR requirements stipulated by the Central bank. Hence, call money market is also known as 'Inter-bank market' or 'Inter bank loan market'.

Participants in Call Market :

- RBI (Central bank),

- Banks,

- Financial institutions,

- Primary dealers,

- Term Money refers to Money lent for 15 days or more in the Inter-Bank Market.

2. **Treasury Bills :**

- Treasury bills are an instrument for sale and purchase of short-term government securities.

- Treasury bills are promissory notes or financial bills issued by the RBI on behalf of the Government of India.
- Treasury bills (T-bills) offer short-term investment opportunities, of upto one year.
- They are useful in managing short-term liquidity.
- Default risk is absent in case of T-bills as these are issued by the Government. As a result, they have become very popular.
- Banks are the major buyers of T-bills as they are eligible for inclusion in SLR.
- Government of India issues the following three types of treasury bills through auctions :

(a)   91-day T-bills,

(b)   182-day T-bills.

(c)   364-day T-bills.

Amount :

- Treasury bills are available for a minimum amount of ₹ 25,000 and in multiples of ₹ 25,000.
- Treasury bills are issued at a discount and are redeemed at face value/par value..
- For example, a Treasury bill of face value ₹ 100 might be issued at ₹ 97 (a discount of ₹ 3. However, on maturity of this T-bill, the investor will receive ₹ 100 (face value/par value). ₹ 3 is thus an interest for the investor.

3. **Commercial Paper :**

- Commercial papers are issued by corporations with a high credit rating.
- They are issued for meeting short-term requirements such as payroll expenses, operating expenses, and current assets.
- For the corporate, Commercial papers serve as an alternative to bank borrowing.
- Infact, corporate can borrow at better interest rates through the Commercial papers

Maturity :

- Typically 1 to 270 days.

Participants :

- Large corporates,
- Mutual Funds,
- Pension Funds,
- Commercial Banks,

- Government,
- Non financial corporations.

4. **Certificate of Deposits (CD's) :**

- A CD is a negotiable money market instrument issued by a commercial bank in dematerialized form for a specified period of time at a market determined discount rate.
- The face value is payable on maturity by the issuing bank.
- CD's are issued by banks and financial institutions to individuals, corporations, trusts, funds and associations.
- A Certificate of Deposit is a time deposit product commonly offered to consumers by banks.
- Sometimes, a bank may not have enough funds to provide a loan so it takes the help of CDs to bridge this shortfall.
- They are issued at a discount rate freely determined by the issuer and the market/investors

Maturity :

- Maturity period of CD's ranges from 7 days to 1 year.
- Being negotiable instruments, CDs are freely transferable by endorsement and delivery.

Participants :

(a) Banks and Financial institutions (issuers),
(b) Individuals, corporations, NRI's (Investors).

Amount :

- Banks have the freedom to issue CDs depending on their funding requirements.
- CD's are issued in multiples of ₹ 1 lakh thereafter.

Reserve Requirements :

- Banks have to maintain appropriate reserve requirements, i.e., Cash Reserve Ratio (CRR) and Statutory Liquidity Ratio (SLR), on the issue price of the CDs.

Example for Understanding the concept of Certificate of Deposits :

- Suppose, ABC Corporation wishes to borrow ₹ 10 crore by next week from a bank. But though the bank agrees to provide a loan, it realizes that it has only ₹ 7 crore at present. The bank does not wish to lose him to another bank. So the bank asks him to come back later to collect the loan amount, at (say) 17%.

- The bank uses its corporate relationships to borrow. The rate of interest offered by the bank to the corporate institutions would be higher than that of the regular fixed deposits. Thus money is received by the bank and is offered to ABC Corporation

5. **Money Market Mutual Fund (MMMF) :**

- Money Market Mutual Fund" means a scheme of a mutual fund which has been set-up with the objective of investing exclusively in money market instruments"- (SEBI).
- It is a mutual fund that is required by law to invest in low-risk securities.
- The objective of Money Market Mutual Fund is to provide investors with highest possible current income, alongwith preservation of capital and liquidity from investing in a diversified portfolio of short-term money market securities.
- A money market mutual fund offers the easiest way for individuals to gain access to the money market.

  Features:
(a) Low risk.
(b) High liquidity.
(c) Preservation of capital.
(d) Diversified portfolio of short-term money market securities.
- Money Market Mutual Funds typically invest in money market instruments such as Certificates of deposit, Commercial paper of companies, Government securities (T-bills), or Securities which are having a high liquidity and a low risk.

6. **Inter Corporate Deposits (ICD) :**

- Inter corporate deposits represent an unsecured loan extended by one corporate to another.
- Corporates with surplus funds to lend to those corporate, who are in need of funds.
- As ICD's are unsecured instruments, the risk associated is higher and hence, higher interest rates are offered for ICD.
- The rate at which the corporate would be able to borrow funds depends upon the short-term credit rating of the corporate .

  Features of ICD :
(a) Cash rich companies provide credit to low rated, cash starved companies.

(b)   Unsecured loans.

(c)   Higher Interest rates as compared to bank rates.

(d)   Higher risk.

- Corporates borrow in ICD market because :

(a)   To meet their requirement for short maturity funds at competitive rates.

(b)   Unsecured instruments and hence, less formalities.

(c)   Better interest rates as compared to bank loans.

(d)   Avoid the hassles that are encountered while applying for a bank loan.

(e)   To avail immediate capital for short-term requirements.

Advantages of ICD to the Investors:

(a)   Higher Interest Rate.

(b)   Increased yield on the investment.

7.   CBLO (Collateralized Borrowing and Lending Obligation) :

- CBLO is a money market instrument that represents an obligation between a borrower and a lender. This obligation is with regards to the terms and conditions of a loan.

- The financial entities who are restricted from participating in the interbank call money market in India use CBLO to participate in the short-term money markets.

- In India, Collateralized Borrowing and Lending Obligations (CBLOs) is a money market segment, operated by the Clearing Corporation of India Ltd (CCIL).

- CBLO is basically, a discounted instrument available in electronic book entry form for the maturity period ranging from one day to one year.

- In terms of functioning and objectives, the CBLO market is quite similar to the call money market.

- In the CBLO market, financial entities can access short-term loans. However, this loan is availed by providing prescribed securities as collateral, which is in contrast to the call money market.

- Eligible securities that can be provided as a collateral are Central Government securities like Treasury Bills, and such other securities as specified by the CCIL.

- Borrowers in CBLO deposit the required amount of eligible securities with the CCIL.

- For trading purposes, the CCIL does order matching(matches the borrowing and lending orders) submitted by the members.

- Borrowers have to pay interest to the lenders in accordance with the bid.
- Several financial entities such as Banks (nationalized, private, foreign and co-operatived banks), NBFC, Insurance Companies, Mutual Funds, Pension funds, Primary Dealers, Corporates are eligible for membership to CBLO.

2.5 ROLE OF CENTRAL BANK IN MONEY MARKET

Introduction

- A central bank refers to an independent monetary authority at a national level that formulates monetary policy, regulates banks and certain financial institutions.
- The central bank prints the national currency, and hence possesses a monopoly in increasing the monetary base in the country.
- The main objectives of the central bank are to prevent high inflation, provide economic growth and to stabilize the nation's currency.
- At the same time, the objectives of the central bank are aligned with the nation's long-term policy goals. The central bank tries to achieve these objectives, basically, through altering the money supply in the economy.
- The central bank is free of political influence in its day-to-day operations.
- In India, the central bank of the country is RBI (Reserve Bank of India).
  RBI regulates:
1. Commercial Banks,
2. Money market,
3. Foreign exchange market.

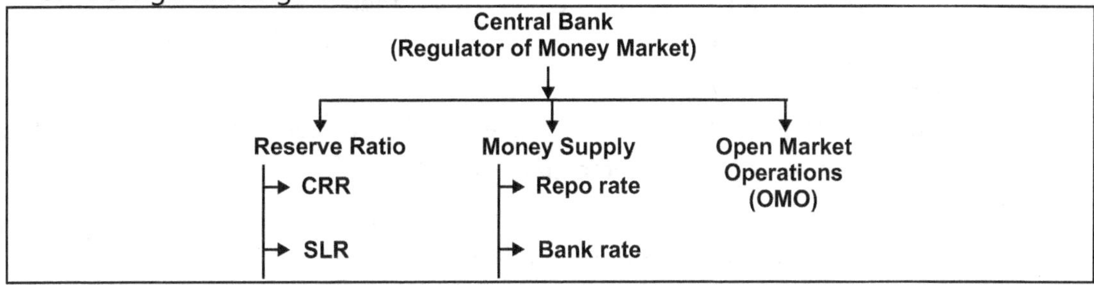

Fig. 2.4 : Central Bank- Regulator of Money Market

RBI influences money market in the following ways:

Central banks affect economic growth by controlling the liquidity in the financial system. They have three major monetary policy tools to achieve this objective.

1. The central bank sets a required reserve ratio, which would restrict the ability of the commercial banks to increase the money supply by loaning out money.
   - If the central bank raises this reserve requirement, the banks will have to create fewer deposits and make fewer loans .
   - Basically, the RBI has got 2 main tools in this regard.
   (a) Cash reserve ratio (CRR),
   (b) Statutory Liquidity Ratio (SLR).

(a) Cash Reserve Ratio (CRR) :
   - It refers to a portion of deposits which banks have to keep/maintain with the RBI, in the form of cash.
   - So when CRR is increased, banks have to keep more money with RBI(than before), i.e. Money supply is reduced ,leading to increase in interest rates in the money market.
   - When CRR is decreased, banks have to keep less money with RBI (than before) i.e. Money supply is increased, leading to decrease in interest rates in the money market.

(b) Statutory Liquidity Ratio (SLR) :
   - It refers to a portion of their deposits which bank has to keep with itself as liquid assets (Gold, approved govt. securities etc.)
   - So when SLR is increased, banks have to keep more money in liquid assets and less money is available for giving loans/credit(than before), i.e. Money supply is reduced.
   - When SLR is decreased, banks have to keep less money in liquid assets and hence, more money is available for giving loans/credit (than before), i.e. Money supply is increased.

2. The supply of money can also be changed by the central bank by adjusting the interest rate at which the commercial banks borrow money (from the Central bank).
   - Basically, the RBI has got 2 main tools in this regard.
   (a) Repo rate,
   (b) Bank rate.

(a) Repo Rate :
   - Repo rate refers to the rate at which banks can borrow short-term money from RBI (via selling their Government securities and agreeing to repurchase them).

- So, when Repo rate is increased, the cost of borrowing funds for bank is increased, which leads them to borrow less or increase interest rate. In other words, Money supply is reduced.
- When Repo rate is decreased, the cost of borrowing funds for bank reduces, which leads them to borrow more or decrease interest rate. In other words, Money supply is increased.

(b) Bank Rate :

- Bank rate refers to the rate at which banks borrow long-term funds from RBI.
- So, when this rate is increased, the cost of borrowing funds for bank is increased, which leads them to borrow less or increase interest rate. In other words, Money supply is reduced.
- When Bank rate is decreased, the cost of borrowing funds for bank reduces, which leads them to borrow more or decrease interest rate.

3. Open Market Operations :

- The central bank can also alter the money supply through its open market operations.
- It refers to the buying and selling of Govt. securities in the open market by RBI, in order to control the volume of credit in an economy.
- So, when RBI buys more of Govt. securities through OMO ,banks sell it to RBI and get money, which can be used by banks to extend credit in the economy. In other words, Money supply is increased.
- When RBI sells more of Govt. securities through OMO ,banks buy it from RBI and the money available to banks for extending credit gets reduced.
- Various tools in the hand of the Central bank discussed above allows it to influence the money supply through the financial base.
- The monetary base will be affected causing the money supply to modify.

2.6 REFORMS IN INDIAN MONEY MARKET

Even though the money market in India does not satisfy the criteria of developed money market, it must be noted that RBI (regulator of Indian money market), alongwith government has been taking various measures to strengthen Indian money market, and make it at par with those of developed countries.

- Most of these measures draw from the recommendations of the Sukhamoy Chakraborty Committee on the "Review of the Working of the Monetary system" and the Narasimham Committee report on the working of the Financial System in India.
- Below are the major reforms in money market undertaken over the past years:

(1) Remission of Stamp Duty :

- Stamp duty on bills was considered a major administrative constraint in the use of bill system. Hence, in August 1989, the Government remitted the stamp duty.
- However, this measure failed to induce use of commercial bills.

(2) Deregulation of Money Market Interest Rates :

- With effect from 1st May,1989, RBI deregulated money market interest rates.
- Removing the interest ceiling on money rates made them flexible and imparted transparency to transactions in the money market.
- Deregulation of interest rates helps banks to accustom to better pricing of assets and liabilities and to the need to manage interest rates across their balance sheet

(3) Introduction of New Money Market Instruments :

Certificate of Deposits :

- In 1988-89,Certificate of deposits were introduced in Indian Money Market. In 1996-97, RBI modified norms and guidelines for these instruments.
- CD's give a greater flexibility to investors in employment of their short-term funds.

Treasury Bills :

- In 1992-93, 364 days treasury bills were introduced.

Commercial Paper :

- In March 1989, RBI announced new scheme of commercial paper.
- Its guidelines came into effect from January 1990.

(4) Introduction of Repo and Reverse Repo :

- Repo and reverse Repo are the major monetary tools in the hands of RBI to tackle inflationary problem.
- In Repo, the borrower borrows money via giving some securities, and undertake a commitment to purchase back these securities after the specified period at a pre-determined price.

- Reverse Repo is opposite of Repo, wherein the lender lends against the securities with the commitment to take back the securities from the borrower against the payment at a specified price.
- From 1998-99, 3-4 days repos and 1 day repos are available.
- RBI also instituted a new marginal standing facility from which scheduled commercial banks can borrow overnight funds.

(5) Setting-up of DFHI (Discount and Finance House of India) :

- DFHI was incorporated in 1988, jointly by RBI and Public Sector Banks and all India Finance Institutions.
- This was the start of significant institutional development and procedural reforms aimed at developing a strong secondary market in government securities.
- DFHI was established with an objective to facilitate the smoothening of short term liquidity imbalances by developing an active money market.
- DFHI was also meant to integrate the various systems of money market.
- In 1992, DFHI started buying and selling Government securities to a limited extent, with a view to develop a secondary market in Government securities.
- DFHI buys bills and other short-term papers from banks and financial institutions and provides short-term investment opportunity to banks.

(6) Introduction of Money Market Mutual Funds :

- Evolution of mutual funds in Indian money market can be tracked in 3 phases, viz.;
  Phase 1 : Establishment Unit Trust of India(UTI), a monopoly in mutual funds industry.
  Phase 2 : Public sector banks and financial institutions were allowed to set-up their mutual funds.
  Phase 3 : Mutual fund industry was opened for entry to private sector
- In 1992 , Money Market Mutual Funds was announced to bring it within in the reach of individuals.
- These funds have been introduced by financial institutions and banks.

(7) Developing Call Money Market :

- The call money market is basically an inter-bank market.
- From 1971 till 1990 ,only UTI and LIC were allowed to operate as lenders.
- After 1990, RBI allowed other financial institutions also to participate in call money market.

- Till 1984, the call rates were administered by Indian Bank's Association. Now, it is decided by market forces.

(8) Strengthening of Institutional Infrastructure :

- Institutional infrastructure has been strengthened with a host of institutions and systems as given below :

(a) Setting up of DFHI.

(b) System of Primary Dealers (PDs) and that of Satellite Dealers (SDs).

(c) Establishment of Securities Trading Corporation of India (STCI) in 1994, to provide better market and liquidity for dated securities, and to hold short-term money market assets like treasury bills.

(d) Transparent and screen based trading in all types of debt instruments, introduced by NSE.

(9) Permission to Foreign Institutional Investors (FII) :

- FII's are allowed to operate in all dated government securities.

- From 1998-99, they have been permitted to buy treasury Bills within approved debt ceiling.

- With the slew of above measures , Indian money market has become more progressive, advanced, solvent and vibrant.

- Moreover, these measures have also been a contributing factor to the development of secondary market

   Difference between Money Market and Capital Market :

- We have seen in the earlier chapter that financial market can either be a Money Market where extremely liquid financial instruments are traded or a Capital Market where buying and selling in securities are done to raise long-term funds for the issuing entity.

- There are similarities as well as differences between capital markets and money markets.

- From the issuer's (seller's) viewpoint, both these markets help in maintaining adequate levels of funding for the business.

- The objective of the issuer to access each market depends on their liquidity needs and time horizon.

- Similarly, investors (buyers) have different reasons for investing in each market:

- Capital markets offer higher-risk, higher returns investments, while money markets offer low-risk, low returns investments.
- Basically the difference between the capital markets and money markets is related to the time horizon.
- Capital markets are for long-term investments.
- Companies are selling stocks and bonds in order to borrow money from their investors to restructure their company or to purchase fixed assets.
- On the other hand, money markets are more of a short term borrowing or lending market where banks and financial institutes borrow and lend with each other.
- Also, the instruments commonly used for raising finance differ in both these markets.
- In the capital markets, the common financial instruments used are stocks and bonds.
- In the money markets, the most common financial instruments used are commercial paper and certificates of deposits.

Basis	Money Market	Capital Market
(1) Meaning :	In this type of financial market, Trading of short-term securities takes place.	In this type of financial market, Trading of long-term securities takes place.
(2) Common Financial Instruments Used :	Treasury Bills, Commercial Papers, Certificate of Deposit.	Shares, Debentures, Bonds.
(3) Risk :	Low.	High.
(4) Returns Expected :	Lower.	Higher.
(5) Time Horizon :	Less than 1 year.	More than 1 year.
(6) Liquidity :	High liquidity as these are short-term instruments.	Low liquidity.
(7) Purpose :	The purpose of issuing money market instruments is to meet the short-term credit needs of business.	The purpose of issuing capital market instruments is to meet the long-term credit needs of business.

Basis	Money Market	Capital Market
(8) Nature :	Not well organized.	Well organized.
(9) Control :	Rate of interest is controlled by central bank of the country (RBI in India's case).	In capital markets, interest and dividend rate depends on demand and supply of securities and stock market's conditions.
(10) Regulator :	Money market in India is regulated by RBI.	Capital market in India is regulated by SEBI.
(11) Major Participants :	Commercial banks like SBI, ICICI Bank, and other financial institutions like UTI , LIC and other financial institutions.	Public and Private Ltd. Companies and Investors (Retail as well as institutional).

Questions for Discussion

1. Explain in detail the concept of Money market.
2. Explain the Structure and Components of Money Market in India.
3. Describe the various Participants/Players in the Indian Money Market.
4. Explain the different Money Market Instruments.
5. Explain the Role of Central Bank in Money Market.
6. List out the various Reforms in Indian Money Market.
7. **Write short notes on :**
(A) Treasury Bill.
(B) Certificate of Deposits (CD).
(C) Commercial Papers (CP).
(D) CBLO.
(E) MMMF's.
(F) Call Money Market.
(G) Unorganised Money Market.
(H) RBI and Money Market.
(I) Indigenous bankers.
(J) Moneylenders.

Chapter **3**...

Capital Market

> *"Money doesn't create man but it is the man who created money."*
> **- Warren Buffet**

Contents ...

Learning Objectives...

After studying this chapter, the student should understand:

• Concept of Capital Market.

• Components of Capital Market-Primary Market and Secondary Market.

• Function and Importance of Capital Markets.

• Primary Market Operations through the process of IPO.

• Secondary Market Operations and Stock exchanges (BSE,NSE).

• Capital Market Instruments - Preference Shares, Equity Shares, Non-voting Shares, Convertible Cumulative Debentures (CCD),Fixed Deposits, Debentures and Bonds, Global Depository Receipts, American Depository receipts, Global Debt Instruments.

• Role of SEBI in Capital Market.

3.1 INTRODUCTION TO CAPITAL MARKET

- It is a market for securities where corporates and governments can raise long-term funds.
- By long-term, it means a market, which provides funds for a period longer than a year.
- Through Capital markets, instruments such as stocks and bonds are issued for the medium-term and long-term.
- Capital markets help channelize surplus funds from savers to the institutions which can invest these funds for productive purposes.
- The prime role of this market is to make investment from investors who have surplus funds to the ones who are having a deficit (shortage) of funds.

Definition:

> *"Capital market is a market where buyers and sellers engage in trade of financial securities like bonds, stocks, etc. Participants such as individuals and institutions undertake the buying / selling."* **- (Economic Times)**

- The stock exchanges along, and other intermediaries provide the necessary platform for trading in secondary market and for clearing and settlement.
- Capital markets are regulated by SEBI. SEBI prescribed the regulatory framework for trading, clearing and settlement of securities.

Financial Instrument Traded in Capital Markets :

- The different Financial Instruments that are traded in the capital markets are:
1. Equity instruments.
2. Debt instruments.
3. Foreign exchange instruments.
4. Derivative instruments.

Participants in Capital Market :

- Various Participants in Capital Markets are:
1. Individual Investors.
2. Institutional investors such as pension funds, insurance companies and mutual funds.
3. Governments.
4. Corporates.
5. Banks and financial institutions.

- Capital markets are important for the functioning of an economy, since capital is must for generating economic output.
- Even the size of a nation's capital markets has been found to be directly proportional to the size of its economy.
- Thus, it can be seen that, the United States of America (USA), the world's largest economy, has the biggest and deepest capital markets.
- Due to information technology, the trading platform of the stock exchange is accessible from anywhere in the country via its trading terminals.
- Capital market helps in capital formation and creation of liquidity.
- Risks of investing in Capital market are high because:
1. Dealing is in long-term securities.
2. Fluctuating prices.
3. Illogical reaction of markets to an economic news or rumors.
4. Speculation.
5. Bond market is risky due to interest rate changes.

3.2 COMPONENTS OF CAPITAL MARKET

- Capital market is broadly divided into two major segments on the basis of new issue or trading of old securities, viz.,
1. Primary market,
2. Secondary market.

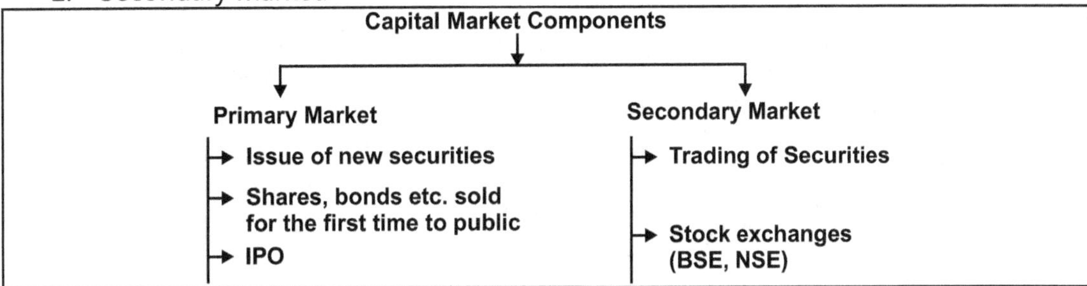

Fig. 3.1 : Components of Capital Market

1. Primary Market :

- It is the market for issuing new securities and hence called the 'New Issue Market'.

- In this market, shares, debentures and other securities are sold for the first time for collecting long-term capital.

Definition :

> *"Primary Market is the part of capital market where issue of new securities takes place."*

- First time sales of equity takes place through primary market.
- As the flow of funds in capital markets is from savers to borrowers (industries), it helps directly in the capital formation.
- Money collected from this market is generally used by the corporate for the purposes of modernization, upgradation, business expansion, setting-up new business units etc.
- Primary market has no particular place.
- Primary market comes before secondary market.
- Many small and medium scale businesses enter the primary market to raise money from the public to expand their businesses. They sell their securities to the public via the process of Initial Public Offering [IPO].
- Following methods can be used to raise capital in the primary market:

(a) Public Issue,

(b) Offer For Sale,

(c) Private Placement,

(d) Right Issue,

(e) Electronic IPO.

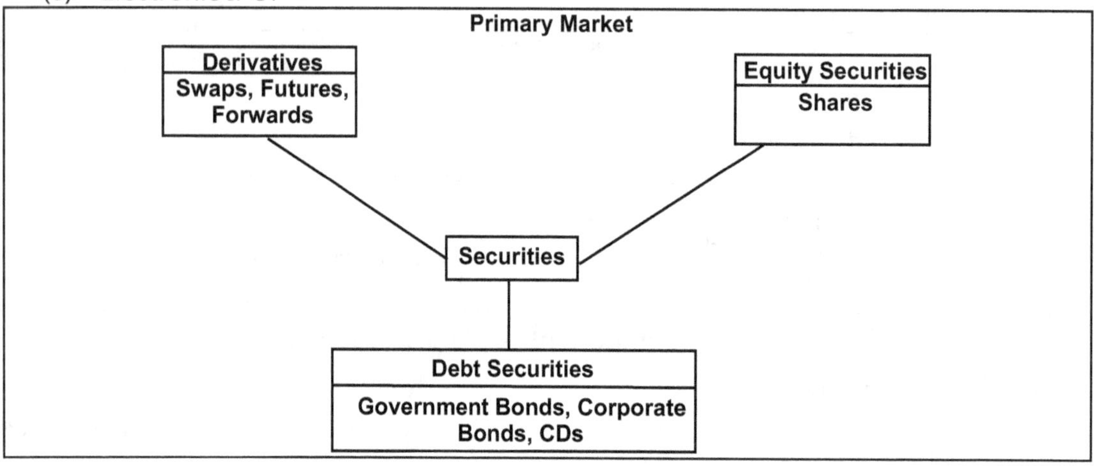

Fig. 3.2 : Primary Market

2. Secondary Market :

- It refers to a financial market, which facilitates trading of securities that have already been issued in an initial private or public offering.
- For example, if one wants to buy shares of Infosys today, he will have to buy them from secondary market.

Definition :

> *"The Secondary Market is the market in which existing securities are resold or traded."*

- The transactions of the secondary market are generally done through the mechanism of stock exchange.
- There are 24 stock exchanges in India.
- Thus, in secondary markets, securities that have been previously issued are resold. In other words, securities are sold and transferred from one investor or speculator to another
- The Secondary market is also known as 'After Market', or 'Stock Market'.
- The main purpose of the secondary market is to create liquidity in securities.
- Secondary Market comes after Primary Market and has a particular place.
- The two major secondary markets of India :

(a) Bombay Stock Exchange (BSE),

(b) National Stock Exchange (NSE).

Linkages between Primary Market and Secondary Market:

- Arrival of new issues affects prices in the secondary market.
- Secondary market depends on the primary market as regards to having the number of securities to trade.
- The secondary market provides a benchmark for the determination of prices of new issues.
- A dynamic and well-developed secondary market is essential for a vibrant primary market.

Difference between Primary Markets and Secondary Markets:

- Primary and secondary markets refer to two different types of marketplaces where investors and traders trade financial securities such as stocks, bonds, debentures etc.

- A primary market is a marketplace where investors can buy a new issue of a security.
- For example, company XYZ comes up with an IPO wherein issue price is ₹200.
- Investors can buy through the IPO at this price and purchase it directly from the issuing company. After this, the stock begins to trade on the secondary market.
- In the secondary market, trading of securities between investors takes place.
- The securities issued in primary markets are traded here.
- Investors and traders engage in market activity through different exchanges, such as the BSE, NSE, and NASDAQ.
- Investors' trade on the secondary market amongst each other and the issuing company is not involved here.
- Suppose Company XYZ had an IPO that first traded on the primary market. Investors and traders who buy or sell shares of Company XYZ are interacting with other investors that own the stock or want to own the stock.
- Therefore, if an investor wants to purchase shares of Company XYZ, he would enter his order through his brokerage firm, and his order would be executed at the best current offer price.

	Primary Market	**Secondary Market**
(1)	Securities are offered for the first time for the purpose of receiving public subscription.	Securities issued in secondary market are dealt between the investors.
(2)	Freshly issued shares.	Formerly issued shares are traded.
(3)	Trading of a security can be done only once.	Trading of a security can be done multiple times.
(4)	Participants include company and investors.	Participants include investors only.
(5)	Intermediaries generally include underwriters.	Intermediaries generally include brokers.
(6)	Fixed price of securities.	Price of securities fluctuate depending on demand and supply.

3.3 FUNCTIONS AND IMPORTANCE OF CAPITAL MARKET

- Capital market, which provides a platform for companies to raise funds on a long-term basis, plays a pivot role in the economy.
- It helps in mobilising resources, and diverting them in productive channels.
- Its functions are stated below:

1. Economic Growth:

- The capital market smoothens and accelerates the process of economic growth.
- Through stock markets, banks and other financial entities, resources are allocated rationally in accordance with the development needs of the country.
- This, in turn, results in the expansion of trade and industry in public and private sectors, thereby promoting balanced economic growth in the country.

2. Mobilisation of Funds:

- Capital markets facilitate transfer of financial resources from surplus areas to deficit areas.
- Through several capital market instruments, savings of surplus units (Individuals and Households) are channelized to the deficit units (Industries and Government) which utilise funds for investment in plants, buildings, machinery, purchase and upgradation of technology, etc.

3. Facilitates Raising Long-term Funds:

- Capital market enables corporates and the government to raise long-term funds, which can be utilized for projects, or investments of a long tenure.
- Funds are raised from both domestic markets and foreign markets.

4. Channelize Saving to Productive Uses:

- Capital market helps in channelizing idle funds from households for investments in the productive channels of an economy.
- Avaialbility of funds to industrial sector in turn raises the output and employment level in a country.

5. Helps in Capital Formation:

- Capital markets facilitate mobilization of idle resources to industrial sector, thereby increasing the existing stock of capital in the economy. It thus helps in capital formation.

- Specifically, primary markets enable transfer of savings of the household sector to industries and government.
- People with surplus money invest their savings in shares, debentures and securities of industries and governments.

6. **Provision of Investment Avenue :**

- Capital market provides an investment avenue for investors who wish to invest resources for long-term, alongwith good returns.
- These returns are in the form of dividends, interest rates, capital appreciation through a variety of Capital market instruments such as equity share, preference shares, debentures etc.

7. **Regulation :**

- Funds mobilized through capital markets are directed in a qualitative manner for productive purposes.
- Additionally, interest of investors in Capital market are protected by the regulator of Capital markets i.e.; SEBI.

8. **Savings to Investments :**

- The surplus money or savings of the people are converted into investments through diverse capital market instruments such as shares, debentures, bonds, etc.

9. **Opportunity for Foreign Investors:**

- Capital markets provide an opportunity to Foreign Institutional Investors (FII) and NRI's to invest in Indian market.
- They can invest in Indian securities of Equity as well as debt nature, and earn more returns as compared to their home country.

10. **Liquidity :**

- Liquidity refers to the ease and speed with which assets can be converted into cash.
- Through capital market, investors can convert their securities into cash, and when they need ,by selling these securities.

3.4 PRIMARY MARKET OPERATIONS

- Primary market is meant for issuing new securities.
- Many small and medium scale businesses enter the primary market to raise money from the public to expand their businesses.

- They sell their securities to the public via the process of Initial Public Offering [IPO].

IPO (Initial Public Offering) :

- A company unlisted on the stock exchange(BSE or NSE) makes either a fresh issue or offers sale of its existing securities(shares) or both for the first time to public, through the process of IPO.

Fig. 3.3 : IPO Process

IPO Process :

- IPO involves a number of steps as listed below:

1. Appointment of Merchant Banker/Lead Managers :

- Merchant banks provide advise on the timing, size and price of the issue.

- In case of IPO, they help the client organization in getting its shares listed on the stock exchange.

- They act as manager to the issue, and help in accepting applications, allotment of securities, and appointing underwriters and brokers to the issue.

- They conduct road shows and provide sales pitch for the company to sell their shares.
- Lead managers even help the companies in creating draft document (DRHP) and getting it approved by SEBI.

2. **Appointment of Underwriter :**

- An Entity which is in the business of evaluating and taking over other people's risk for a fee in return is called as a 'Underwriter'.
- This fee can be called by different names as commission, premium, underwriting spread etc.
- In order to ensure full subscription or the stipulated minimum subscription of the issue, companies take underwriting services to underwrite (take risk) of the issue amount.
- Merchant bankers can underwrite issues and also assist companies in tying up with other underwriters
- For example, an investment bank/merchant bank underwrites an Initial Public Offer (IPO) or a bond issue when it buys the shares or bonds from the issuer.
- It undertakes the risk of having to sell them to individual or institutional investors to recover its investment, or in cases, even hold them, if no buyer is found.

3. **Price Discovery through Book Building Process :**

- In the process of IPO, 'Book building' activity helps to determine price and in demand discovery.
- The public offer of equity shares of a company is marketed offering several price ranges, instead of a fixed price. The book for the IPO is open for a certain time period (normally 5 days), during which the bids are solicited from investors at various prices in the price band (Price band refers to a range of prices, say, 100-120 is a price band which offers price ranges from 100, 101, 102 .... 119, 120).
- The issue price is then determined after the bid closure based on demand generated in the process.
- For example, the company can keep the price band as 100-120 (After consultation with merchant bankers and underwriters) for issuing 1 lakh shares. Here, the lowest price in the price band ₹ 100 is called as floor price, and the highest price, ₹ 120 is called as cap price.

- The investors will submit their bids during the period when the book for IPO is open. Suppose, the number of investors bid for these prices as given in the table shown.

Price	No. of Shares bidded
120	30,000
119	15,000
118	50,000
117	10,000
116	

- The issue will be priced at ₹ 117. As the required 1 lakh shares have been now bidded till this price. The shares will thus, be issued at a price of ₹ 117 / share.

4. Appointment of Registrars :

- The registrar basically provides administrative support to the issue process.
- Registrar process the application forms received from investors, tabulate the money collected during the issue ,make reconciliation of bank accounts and make the allotment of shares to investors.

5. Appointment of the Brokers to the Issue :

- Recognized members of the Stock exchanges are appointed as brokers to the issue.
- They perform the function of marketing and selling bulk shares, in exchange for a brokerage (around 1%).
- Basically, brokers provide information to investors about the issue and distributes issue stationery at retail investor level.

6. Registration of the Offer Document (DRHP) to SEBI :

- The company making an issue must file copy of the Draft Red-Herring Prospectus (DRHP) with SEBI.
- The draft prospectus filed is a public document which contains details of the Company such as:

(a) Information about Company's Business and the sector,

(b) Promoter's background and Management information,

(c) Terms of the issue,

(d) Project details,

(e)   Financing details,

(f)   Past and projected financial reports,

(g)   Projected profitability,

(h)   Risk factors related to company.

- SEBI gives its observation and recommends necessary changes.
- SEBI uploads the draft prospectus document on its website which is open for general public to be viewed.

7. **Filing of Prospectus with the Registrar of Companies (ROC) :**

- The company going for IPO must filed its prospectus with the ROC of the state where the registered office of the company is located.
- The prospectus must be accompanied by the copies of the agreements entered into with the Merchant bankers, Underwriters, Bankers, Registrars and Brokers to the issue .

8. **Printing and Dispatch of Applications Forms :**

- The application forms, alongwith the company's prospectus are printed and dispatched to all the merchant bankers, underwriters, brokers to the issue for further distribution to prospects.

9. **Filing of the Initial Listing Application with Stock Exchange/s :**

- The initial listing application is sent to the Stock exchanges where the issue is proposed to be listed (BSE and NSE in India), alongwith the listing fee.
- The application gives the details of the company, stating the intent of the company to get its shares listed on the Exchange.

10. **Statutory Announcement :**

- An abridged version of the prospectus and the start and close dates of the IPO are published in major English dailies and vernacular newspapers.

11. **Processing of Applications and Allotment of Shares :**

- After the IPO is closed, all the application forms are scrutinized and tabulated.
- If found okay, shares are allotted against these applications.
- The list of eligible allottees is finalized by the Registrar.
- He ensures that the crediting of shares to the Demat Accounts of the applicants is done and the dispatch of refund orders to those applicable are sent.

12. Listing of the Issue :

- The shares after having been allotted have to be listed compulsorily on at least 1 stock exchange.

Major Primary Market Operations :

- Thus, looking at the IPO process in Primary market, the following major operations in Primary market can be identified:

1. Appointment of merchant banker/lead banker,
2. Appointment of underwriter,
3. Book building process (for price discovery of shares),
4. Appointment of Registrars,
5. Appointment of Brokers,
6. Registration of the Offer Document (DRHP) to SEBI,
7. Filing of prospectus with the Registrar of Companies (ROC),
8. Printing and Dispatch of Application Forms,
9. Filing of the initial listing application with Stock Exchange/s,
10. Statutory announcement,
11. Processing of applications and allotment of shares,
12. Listing of the Issue.

3.5 SECONDARY MARKET OPERATIONS

- The transactions of the secondary market are generally done through the mechanism of stock exchange.
- The major ones in this regard are Bombay Stock Exchange (BSE) and National Stock Exchange (NSE).
- Though stock market predominantly deal in the equity shares of companies, debt instruments like bonds and debentures are also traded in the stock market.
- Well regulated and active stock market promotes capital formation.
- The main purpose of the secondary market is to create liquidity in securities.

Stock Exchanges in India :

Definitions:

> **1. *The Securities Regulation Act of 1956* :** *"An association, organization, or an individual which is established for the purpose of assisting, regulating, and controlling business in buying, selling and dealing in securities".*

> **2.** **_Husband and Dockerary_** **:** _"Stock exchanges are privately organized markets which are used to facilitate trading in securities."_

- A stock exchange is an entity that provides services for stockbrokers and traders to trade financial securities such as stocks and bonds.
- Stock exchanges facilitate issue and redemption of securities and other financial instruments.
- Payment of income and dividends is also done through stock exchanges.

Securities Traded in Stock Exchange :

1. Shares issued by companies,
2. Derivatives,
3. Bonds,
4. Pooled investment products.

Role of Stock Exchanges :

- Economic well-being of the country is reflected by the growth of the stock market, as it performs the following important functions:

1. Raising finance/capital for businesses.
2. Provide a convenient meeting place for sellers and buyer of securities.
3. Increase liquidity of shares.
4. Mobilizing savings for investment purposes.
5. Promoting the habit of savings and investment.
6. Ensures a safe and fair dealing.
7. Dis-semination of information.
8. Facilitating a company's growth.
9. Creating investment opportunities for small investors.
10. Facilitate Government in raising capital for development projects.
11. Serves as a Barometer of the economy.
12. Fair value determination of prices of securities.

- Most of the trading in the Indian stock market takes place on its two stock exchanges, i.e.; Bombay Stock Exchange (BSE) and the National Stock Exchange (NSE).
- Almost all the significant firms in the country are listed on these exchanges.
- NSE enjoys a dominant share in spot trading, and almost a complete monopoly in derivatives trading.

- Both exchanges compete for the order flow that leads to reduced costs, market efficiency, technological advance and innovation.
- Arbitrageurs keeps the prices on the two stock exchanges in a tight range.

Major Participants in Stock Exchanges (Stock Markets) :

1. Retail/ individual investors.
2. Institutional investors (banks, mutual funds, insurance companies, publicly traded corporations).

Regulation of Stock Exchanges :

- In India, the stock exchanges are regulated by SEBI.

Trading :

- Trading at both these exchanges (NSE and BSE) takes place through an open electronic limit order book, in which order matching is done by the trading computer.
- All orders in the trading system are required to be placed through brokers.
- Many of these brokers provide online trading facility to their clients.

Settlement Cycle :

- Settlement in equity markets follow a T+2 rolling settlement. T+2 means that any trade taking place on Monday, gets settled by Wednesday.
- Delivery of shares is made in dematerialized (DEMAT) form.
- Each exchange has its own clearing house, which assumes the settlement risk, and serves as a central counterparty.

Stock Indices :

- The two prominent Indian market indexes are:

(1) Sensex (BSE),

(2) Nifty (NSE).

- Sensex is the oldest market index for equities, with shares of 30 firms listed on the BSE, which represent about 50% of the index's free-float market capitalization.
- Nifty of NSE includes 50 shares listed on the NSE, which represent about 60% of its free-float market capitalization.

Stock Exchanges in India :

- Below is the list of Stock Exchanges in India:

1. Bombay Stock Exchange.

2. National Stock Exchange.
3. Ahmedabad Stock Exchange.
4. Bangalore Stock Exchange.
5. Bhubaneshwar Stock Exchange.
6. Calcutta Stock Exchange.
7. Cochin Stock Exchange.
8. Coimbatore Stock Exchange.
9. Delhi Stock Exchange.
10. Guwahati Stock Exchange.
11. Hyderabad Stock Exchange.
12. Jaipur Stock Exchange.
13. Ludhiana Stock Exchange.
14. Madhya Pradesh Stock Exchange.
15. Madras Stock Exchange.
16. Magadha Stock Exchange.
17. Mangalore Stock Exchange.
18. Meerut Stock Exchange.
19. OTC Exchange Of India Stock Exchange.
20. Pune Stock Exchange.
21. Saurashtra Stock Exchange.
22. Kutch Stock Exchange.
23. Uttar Pradesh Stock Exchange.
24. Vadodara Stock Exchange.

(I) National Stock Exchange of India (NSE):

- Incorporated in 1992, the National Stock Exchange (NSE) is India's leading stock exchange.
- It offers trading in equity, derivatives as well as debt segments.

Vision :

- To continue to be a leader, establish global presence; facilitate the financial well being of people.

Purpose :

- Committed to improve the financial well-being of people.

- NSE was set-up by leading financial institutions in the country to provide a modern, fully automated screen-based trading system with national reach.
- The Exchange has brought about unparalleled transparency, speed & efficiency, safety and market integrity.
- It has set-up facilities that serve as a model for the securities industry in terms of systems, practices and procedures.
- It started operations in 1994, with trading on the wholesale debt market segment.
- Subsequently, it launched the capital market segment in the same year as a trading platform for equities.
- In the year 2000, it launched the futures and options segment for various derivative instruments.
- NSE has a market capitalization of around US$1.7 trillion, making it the world's 12th-largest stock exchange as of March 2015.
- There are more than 2000 companies listed on NSE.
- NSE's flagship index, the CNX Nifty, which consists of 50 stocks, is used extensively by investors in India and around the world as a barometer of the Indian capital markets.
- NSE has played a catalytic role in reforming the Indian securities market in terms of structure, market practices and trading volumes.
- The market today uses state-of-art information technology to provide an efficient and transparent trading, clearing and settlement mechanism.
- In addition, several innovations in products & services have also taken place.
- A few examples are demutualization of stock exchange governance, screen based trading, reduction of settlement cycles, dematerialization and electronic transfer of securities, professionalization of trading members, fine-tuned risk management systems, emergence of clearing corporations to assume counterparty risks, market of debt and derivative instruments .
- NSE was the first exchange in the world to use satellite communication technology for trading, using a client server based system called National Exchange for Automated Trading (NEAT). It processed trades in less than a second.
- The National Stock Exchange has become the first Clearing Corporation in India by the introduction of NSCCL in April 1995.

- In the same year, 1995 July, it has introduced the Investor protection fund which is a very important function introduced by the National Stock Exchange.
- Financial literacy, training and certifications: NSE also conducts online examination and awards certification, under its programmes of NSEs Certification in Financial Markets (NCFM), covering different sectors of financial and capital markets.

Market Segments of NSE :

1. **Whole Sale Debt Market Segment :**
- This is a trading platform for a wide range of fixed income securities that include central government securities, treasury bills, bonds issued by public sector undertakings, floating rate bonds, zero coupon bonds, index bonds, commercial paper, certificate of deposit, corporate debentures and mutual funds.

2. **Capital Market Segment :**
- It provides an efficient and transparent platform for trading in equity shares, preference shares, debentures, exchange traded funds as well as retail Government securities.

3. **Derivatives Segment :**
- It refers to futures and options.
- NSE also provides depository services through its National Depository Services Ltd. (NDSL) arm.

(II) Bombay Stock Exchange Limited (BSE):
- Established in 1875, BSE is Asia's first & fastest Stock Exchange with the speed of 200 microseconds and one of India's leading exchange groups.
- It is located on Dalal Street, Mumbai.

Vision :
- "Emerge as the premier Indian stock exchange with best-in-class global practice in technology, products innovation and customer service".
- Over the past 140 years, BSE has facilitated the growth of the Indian corporate sector by providing it an efficient platform for raising capital.
- BSE provides an efficient and transparent market for trading in equity, debt instruments, derivatives, mutual funds.
- It also provides a platform for trading in equities of Small and Medium Enterprises (SMEs).

- Historically from an open outcry floor trading exchange, BSE switched to an electronic trading system in 1995. This automated, screen-based trading platform is called BSE On Line Trading (BOLT).
- Over 5500 companies are listed on BSE making it world's No. 1 exchange in terms of listed members.
- With a total market capitalization of USD 1.68 Trillion as of March 2015, it is the world's 11th largest stock market by market capitalization.
- BSE's index-SENSEX is India's most widely tracked security indices.
- It is a means to measure overall performance of the exchange.
- The SENSEX is made up of 30 of the most actively traded stocks (shares) in the market. It represents 13 sectors of the economy, and these 30 shares account for half the BSE's market capitalization.
- In 2000, the BSE used this index to open its derivatives market, trading SENSEX futures contracts.
- BSE also provides a host of other services to capital market participants such as risk management, clearing, settlement, market data services and education.
- It has a global reach with customers around the world and a nation-wide presence.
- BSE systems and processes are designed to safeguard market integrity, drive the growth of the Indian capital market and stimulate innovation and competition across all market segments.
- BSE also provides depository services through its Central Depository Services Ltd. (CDSL) arm.
  Summary of BSE :

- India's (as well as Asia's) first stock exchange.
- Index-SENSEX.
- Provides for trading in shares as well as derivatives market.
- Market capitalization of USD 1.68 trillion.
- More than 5,500 listed companies.
- CDSL for depository.
- BOLT for online trading.

(III)   Over the Counter Exchange of India (OTCEI):

- OTCEI was incorporated in 1990, as a Section 25 company under the Companies Act 1956, and is recognized as a stock exchange under Section 4 of the Securities Contracts Regulation Act, 1956.

- OTC Exchange of India has been promoted by the leading financial institutions of the country such as Life Insurance Corporation of India, SBI Capital Markets Limited, ICICI Bank Limited and many more.

Definition:

> *"OTCEI is an electronic stock exchange based in India that is comprised of small- and medium-sized firms looking to gain access to the capital markets. There is no central place of exchange and all trading is done through electronic networks."*

- The Exchange was set-up to aid enterprising promoters in raising finance for new projects in a cost effective manner and to provide investors with a transparent & efficient mode of trading.

- It address the specific needs of small enterprises.

- Over-the-Counter Exchange is the first exchange for small companies. OTCEI provides them with access to public funds at a low cost.

- Over-the-Counter (OTC) or Off-exchange trading is done directly between the two counter-parties, thereby, by-passing any supervision of an exchange.

- It is a floorless market without trading ring and transactions are done through telephone, telex and other such communication means and completed through negotiation.

- OTCEI introduced many novel concepts to the Indian capital markets such as screen-based nationwide trading, sponsorship of companies, market making and script less trading.

- As a measure of success of these efforts, the exchange today has more than 100 listings and has assisted in providing capital for enterprises that have gone on to become successful brands such as VIP Advanta, Sonora Tiles & Brilliant mineral water etc

Need for OTCEI :

1. It provides liquidity to the shares of companies listed on the stock exchange.

2. Small entrepreneurs can raise funds through OTCEI. The funds thus raised aids the growth of these companies.

    Objectives of OTCEI :

1. Provide Liquidity.
2. To simplify the process of buying and selling.
3. To facilitate quick disposal of orders.
4. To provide for a cost-effective method of public sale of new issues.

    Trading Orders :

- Stock exchanges exist to support secondary market operations, i.e. trading of shares.
- In other words, buying and selling of equity shares of companies listed on stock exchange takes place in secondary market.
- Different types of orders can be given by the client which are executed by the broker through his trading terminal.
- These orders are as follows:

1.   Market Order :

- It is an order to buy or sell a security (equity share) immediately.
- This type of order is guaranteed to be executed. However, the execution price is not guaranteed.
- A market order generally gets executed at or near the current bid price (for a sell order), or ask price (for a buy order).

2.   Limit Order :

- It is an order to buy or sell a security at a price specified by the client (trader or investor), or a better price.
- A buy limit order can only be executed at the limit price specified by the client, or lower.
- Conversely, a sell limit order can only be executed at the limit price specified by the client ,or higher.

    Example : A trader or an investor wants to purchase shares of Infosys for no more than ₹ 1000. He can submit a limit order for this amount and this order will only execute if the price of Infosys share is ₹ 1000 or lower.

3.   Stop-loss Order :

- Also referred as a stop order. It is an order to buy or sell a stock once the price of the stock reaches the specified price, known as the stop price.
- The moment the stop price is reached, a stop order becomes a market order.
- Normally, traders use a sell stop-order. A sell stop order is entered at a stop price below the current market price. Traders and investors generally use a sell stop order to limit a loss or protect a profit on a stock they own.
- For example, if the current price of a share of ABC Ltd. is ₹ 100, the trader can give a sell stop-loss order at ₹ 90. In this case, his loss is limited if the share price goes on a downward slope.
- Conversely, a buy stop order is entered at a stop price above the current market price. Traders use a buy stop order in case of short-selling. It helps them to limit a loss ,or protect a profit on a stock that they have sold short.

3.6   CAPITAL MARKET INSTRUMENTS

- Capital Market Instruments refer to the different sources of finance, through which a business enterprise ,or a financial entity, or the Government can raise long-term finance.
- Some are debt sources; whereas some are equity sources. There are such several domestic and international sources.
- Following are the major Capital Market Instruments:
1. Preference Shares,
2. Equity Shares,
3. Non-voting Shares,
4. Debentures,
5. Compulsory Convertible Debentures (CCD),
6. Fixed Deposits,
7. Bonds,
8. American Depository Receipts (ADR),
9. Global Depository Receipts (GDR),
10. Global Debt Instruments (ECB, Eurobond, Foreign bond).
- We will study them in a sequential manner.

1. Preference Shares :

- A fixed dividend is paid to preference shareholders, as stated by the company.
- By preference, we mean that the holder of these shares get preference/priority over equity shares in the following matters :

(a) payment of dividend,

(b) payment of dues on liquidation of the company.

- Preference shareholders have the right to get dividend at a fixed rate.
- Additionally, the preference shareholders get repayment of capital before equity shareholders when the company is liquidated.
- However, the claims of preference shareholders on earnings and assets of the company, in the event of liquidation, rank below creditors of the company.
- In case of preference shares, dividend declaration by the company is not compulsory.
- Dividends may not be paid in a year when profits are not enough and the preference shareholders cannot take legal action against the company for not declaring dividends.
- At the same time, no dividend can be declared on Equity shares, unless dividend on preference shares is declared and paid.
- Preference shareholders do not enjoy voting rights and do not share in the profits of the company
- They are also known as hybrid securities because, they have the qualities of equity shares as well as debt.
- Preference shares exhibit characteristics of Equity like they are to be paid out of distributable profits, preference dividend payment is not obligatory, and preference dividends are not tax-deductible expense.
- Preference shares exhibit characteristics of Debt like fixed rate of dividend, and no voting rights. Moreover, preference shareholders have a claim above equity shareholders in case of dividend payment and winding-up of the company.
- Some experts hence, mention them as 'Quasi-equity'.

Advantages :

(a) Dividend Payment :

- The company has no legal obligation to pay dividends to preference shareholders.
- The company does not face bankruptcy or legal action if preference dividend is skipped.

(b) Control :

- There is no loss of control of the promoters, as preference shareholders do not have voting rights.

Disadvantages :

(a) Expensive :

- Preference share capital is expensive as the dividend paid on preference shares are not tax-deductible expenses.

2. Equity Shares :

- Equity shares are also known as 'Ordinary shares ' or simply ' Shares'.
- As per Companies Act, 2013, a share is a part of unit by which the share capital of a company is divided.
- Company's capital is divided into number of identical units, known as Shares.
- For example, if a company requires a capital of ₹ 10 lakh, it can be divided into equal parts of ₹ 10 each. In other words, a company can issue 1 lakh shares at ₹ 10 each and thereby, raise a capital of ₹ 10 lakh.
- Equity shares, thus, represents the form of fractional or part ownership of the company.
- Equity share capital cannot be redeemed during the lifetime of the company and thus, serves as permanent nature of capital for the company, which has no maturity period.
- Equity shares are the major source of financing for a company.
- Equity share capital is also known as risk capital as the equity shareholders are exposed to greater amounts of risk, but at the same time they have greater opportunities for getting higher returns
- Legally, equity shareholders are the owners of the company.
- They have a voting right in the company matters such as election of director, acquisition etc.
- Equity shareholders are paid dividends out of the profits of the company (or may not be paid), after paying it to the preference shareholders.

Advantages :

(a) Permanent Capital to the Company :

- Since equity shares have no maturity period, they serve as a permanent capital for the company.

(b) Dividends not Compulsory :

- In case of Equity shares, there is no obligation on part of the company to pay dividend.
- If the company earns profit, equity shareholders are eligible for profit. They are also eligible to get dividend otherwise. However, they cannot claim any dividend from the company.

(c) Debt Capacity :

- Equity, including reserves, enhances the capacity of a company to raise finance from debt sources.

Disadvantages:

(a) High Cost :

- Amongst various sources of finance, equity capital's cost is high, as there is a higher risk involved for investors.
- Moreover, the dividends paid to equity shareholders are not tax-deductible like interest paid on loans or debentures

(b) Flotation Costs :

- For raising finance through equity shares, a company appoints a merchant banker, who is paid some commission .
- Thus, Raising finance through equity involves floatation costs.

(c) Controlling Power :

- Raising finance through equity shares will dilute the control of promoters, unless they contribute proportionately to the additional finance raised through equity shares.

3. Non-voting Shares :

- Some companies choose to have multiple classes of shares.
- As the name suggests, Non-voting Shares do not enjoy any voting rights like ordinary shares.
- In other words, Non-voting shares are ordinary shares of a publicly listed corporation, that lack voting rights at the annual general meeting of the company.
- When the founders of a company want to raise new share capital without losing their control of the company, Non-voting shares are issued.
- The voting rights of the founders are retained with their ownership of the original shares.

- Voting issues aside, they have the same rights to profits and company ownership as the equity shares even if, these shares are of inferior class of common stock for a given company. So if, large stakeholders are successful in running the company, this should be of no concern to non-voting shares.
- As it is, a typical retail investor has a very tiny stake in the company. Only if, disproportionate voting rights lead to inferior management against the best interests of shareholders, non-voting shares can be a concern.
- A company may issue non-voting shares to its employees because they want them to be able to benefit from profits or dividends but do not want them to participate in decision making.

4. **Debentures :**

- Debentures are a major source of long-term funds for a company.
- For investors, debentures is a long-term security yielding a fixed rate of interest.
- It is a debt source of finance for the company.
- Debenture refers to a document issued by a company as evidence of debt to the holder, usually arising out of loan and mostly secured by charge.
- In other words, Debentures are issued by a company and secured against assets.
- The debentureholders are the creditors of the company.

   Advantages :

(a) **No interference in Company Matters :**

- The debenture holders cannot interfere in the company matters as they do not have voting rights.

(b) **Low Cost :**

- As the interest payments on debentures are tax deductible expenses, the cost of debentures is likewise low.

   Disadvantages :

(a) **Default might be Costly :**

- Debentureholders can initiate legal proceedings against a company, if it defaults on its principal repayment, and/or interest payments, when these become due.

5. **Compulsory Convertible Debentures (CCD) :**

- Compulsory Convertible Debenture (CCD) is a debt instrument issued by a company, which is convertible into equity shares of such company at a specified time.

- After the CCD's are converted into equity shares, the holder of CCD's automatically becomes a shareholder in the company and is entitled to all the rights of a equity shareholder ,such as voting rights.
- One can simply state that debentures which are to be compulsorily converted into debentures at a specified date are CCD's.
- CCD can therefore be classified as a hybrid security, meaning it is considered neither a pure debt instrument, nor a pure equity instrument.
- According to the Reserve Bank of India (RBI) guidelines, CCDs are treated as equity for all the reporting purposes including financial statements.
- CCDs are however, not treated as part of the share capital of a company, unless they are converted into equity.
- CCD's are required to be fully paid-up, and the price/ conversion formula needs to be determined upfront at the time of issue.
- The whole value of the debenture must be converted into equity till a specified time.
- The company issuing the CCD's decide the compulsory convertible debentures' ratio of conversion at the time of issue.

   Advantages:
- Over the past decade, there has been a spectacular rise in CCD issues, due to the reasons mentioned below:

(a) **Discount :**
- CCDs are generally issued at a discount to the valuation of the next round of investment, since an investor is investing in the nascent stage of the portfolio company .

(b) **Rate of Interest :**
- The interest rate paid on CCD's is generally lower than the rate of interest paid on Non-Convertible Debentures.
- Moreover, the CCDs offer tax rebate.
- The interest paid to a CCD holder is allowed as a deduction at the time of computation of the portfolio company's taxable income.

(c) **Preferential Payment :**
- As CCDs are a hybrid instrument, CCD holder has a preferential right of payment over other stakeholders of the portfolio company ,until the time they are converted to equity shares.

(d) Transparency :

- The terms & conditions of a CCD are decided upfront at the time of their issuance. Moreover, the price/conversion formula of CCDs is also determined at the time of their issue.
- These clear terms and conditions add to transparency for the investor, making CCD a reliable long-term investment vehicle.

(e) Debenture Reserve :

- In case of a Non-Convertible Debenture, the portfolio company is required to create a Debenture Redemption Reserve, execute a debenture trust deed, and appoint a debenture trustee.
- However, the issuance of CCDs does not require any such conditions to be fulfilled by the portfolio company

Disadvantages :

(a) Compliance :

- Issuance of CCDs requires dealing with regular compliance work.

6. Fixed Deposits :

- FD accounts or term deposits are used by financial entities such as banks to mobilize savings of people for a long-term period.
- A fixed rate of interest is paid on these accounts, say 9% p.a.
- The principal is paid only on maturity.
- In a FD, a lumpsum amount is deposited for a fixed term/ tenure during which the amount cannot be withdrawn.
- If the depositor withdraws the money before the completion of the tenure, banks might levy penalty for premature withdrawal.
- This penalty is mostly out of the interest, which depositors get on these fixed deposits.
- In other words, some portion of the interest will not be paid to the depositors.
- Bank provide highest rate of interest on this type of account.
- The interest is paid on a monthly or quarterly or half-yearly or an annual basis.
- TDS is applicable if the amount of interest exceed ₹ 10,000.
- Suppose, a depositor has made a fixed deposit of ₹ 1,00,000 for a period of 1 year, at an interest rate of 10 %. At the end of this period (one year), he will receive ₹ 1,10,000 (Original principal of ₹ 1,00,000 + an interest of ₹ 10,000 at 10

% interest rate). The amount may be slightly higher in case of quarterly compounding.

7. **Bonds :**

- A bond is a fixed income debt instrument, through which a corporate or governmental entity can raise capital for long-term from the investors.
- In other words, Bond represents a loan made by an investor to a borrower (corporate or government entity).
- Bonds are used by corporates, municipalities, states, and sovereign governments to finance projects and operations.
- A bond has a maturity period. At the end of the maturity period, the principal of the loan is due to be paid to the bond owner (investor).
- Besides, interest payments are to be made by the borrower, on fixed or variable terms, and at intervals, and the interest rate specified in the terms.
- The borrower entity (issuer of the bond) issues a bond that includes the terms of the loan, interest payments (coupon/coupon rate) that will be made, and the time at which the principal amount must be paid back to the investor (maturity date).
- At the end of the maturity period, the face value of the bond is paid back to the bond investor.
- Simply speaking, owners/investors of bonds are creditors of the issuer of the bond.
- In many matured markets, corporate and government bonds are publicly traded.
- Bonds are generally, issued at par, or face value. This face value is usually ₹ 100 or ₹1,000 per individual bond.
- In many matured markets, corporate and government bonds are publicly traded.
- The actual market price of a bond then keeps on fluctuating based on several factors i.e. the credit quality of the issuer of the bond, the length of time until expiration, and the coupon rate compared to the general interest rate environment at that time.
- The coupon rate of the bond depends upon the Credit ratings of the bond issuer, which are generated by credit rating agencies like Standard and Poor's, Moody's, and Fitch Ratings.

Example :

- Suppose a bond that was issued with a ₹ 1,000 par value and coupon rate of 10%. The bondholder (investor) will be paid ` 100 in interest income annually (most bond coupons are split in half and paid semi-annually.)
- If the interest rate environment does not change, the price of the bond should remain at its par value. However, if the interest rate environment changes, the bond price will fluctuate as the bond price tends to move inversely with interest rates.
- If interest rates begin to decline and similar debt instruments are now issued with a 8 % coupon, the original bond becomes more valuable as the investors requiring a higher coupon rate will have to pay extra for the bond in order to entice the original owner to sell. As a result, the price of the bond will increase.
- Conversely, if interest rates rise and similar debt instruments are now issued with a 12 % coupon, the 10 % coupon for the original bond is no longer attractive.

Basic Terminologies in Bonds:

(a) Face Value/Par Value :

- The value of bond at maturity.
- Reference amount the bond issuer uses when calculating interest payments.
- Like ₹ 1000.

(b) Coupon Rate :

- Interest rate that the bond issuer will pay on the face value of the bond.
- Expressed as a percentage.
- For example, a 10% coupon rate means that bondholders will receive 10% × ₹ 1,000 face value = ₹100 every year.

(c) Maturity Date :

- Date on which the bond will mature.
- At maturity date, the bond issuer will pay the bondholder the face value of the bond.

8. American Depository Receipts (ADR) :

- American Depositary Receipt (ADR) is a negotiable instrument denominated in US dollar for which ordinary shares(of a non-US security)serves as an underlying.
- ADRs are listed on US stock exchanges, viz. New York Stock Exchange (NYSE), American Stock Exchange (AMEX) or the Nasdaq.
- Infosys has its ADR's listed on NYSE.

- ADR represents an ownership in a non-US security and ADR holder, indeed, has a right to obtain delivery of actual shares, if he desires. Prices of global depositary receipt are based on the values of related shares.
- It was devised in the late 1920s to help American citizens invest in overseas securities and to assist non-US companies wishing to list their security in American Markets.
- ADR's were introduced to overcome the complexities involved in buying shares in foreign countries and the associated risks regarding prices and currency values.
- The company, though, listed in America, will have its revenue and profit denominated in its home currency.

Working of ADR :

- Suppose,1 share of ITC in Indian market trades around ₹ 600, nearly equivalent to 10 Dollars. Citi Bank buys 100 shares of ITC and issues in the ratio 10:1 in US market, means 1 ADR represents 10 ITC shares, i.e. 100 dollars. . Subsequent price will be determined by market forces.

Sponsored ADR's and Unsponsored ADR's:

- Sponsored ADR's involve voluntary entry of company in the American market, and therefore the company needs to file with the SEC.
- The company's ADRs are listed on US stock exchanges, viz. New York Stock Exchange (NYSE), American Stock Exchange (AMEX) or the Nasdaq. Level III sponsored ADRs permit the company to issue shares to raise capital.
- Unsponsored ADR's are often issued by a depositary bank and trade on the over-the- counter (OTC).
- They are issued in accordance with market demand, and the foreign company has no formal agreement with a depositary bank.
- Company does not need to file with the SEC (Securities Exchange Commission) as the company's entry is involuntary.

Advantages of ADR :

(a) **For Individuals :**

(i) Easy and cost-effective way to buy shares in a foreign company.

(ii) Reduced administration costs.

(iii) Avoid foreign taxes on each transaction.

(b) For Foreign Companies :

(i) U.S. exposure.

(ii) Increases visibility of the entity.

(iii) Allowing them to tap capital from American equities markets.

(iv) Increases the share liquidity.

9. Global Depository Receipts (GDR) :

- A global depository receipt is a freely traded negotiable instrument, issued by a depository bank which purchases shares of foreign companies and deposits it on the account.

- GDRs represent ownership of an underlying number of shares of a foreign company and are commonly used by investors in developed markets to invest in companies from emerging markets.

- GDR is denominated in US dollars or Euros, and is listed on non-US stock exchange

- Prices of global depositary receipt are based on the values of related shares.

- GDRs enable a company, or the issuer to access capital from investors outside its home country.

- GDRs are often listed on the Luxembourg Stock Exchange, Frankfurt Stock Exchange, Hong Kong Stock Exchange and the London Stock Exchange.

- Usually, 1 GDR is equal to 10 underlying shares, but any ratio can be used.

Working of GDR :

Suppose 1 share of RIL in Indian market trades around ₹ 1,000, nearly equivalent to 10 Euros. Barclays Bank buys 100 shares of RIL and issues in the ratio 10:1 in foreign market, means 1 GDR represents 10 RIL shares, i.e. 100 Euros. Subsequent price will be determined by market forces.

Advantages of GDR :

(a) For the Investor :

(i) Helps to invest in foreign companies.

(ii) Advantage of emerging market economies.

(iii) Higher transparency and stability.

(iv) GDR's encourage an international shareholder base and provide expatriates living abroad with an easier opportunity to invest in their home countries

(v) Investors' portfolio turns into a global one.

(vi) Investors gain the benefits of diversification, while trading in their own market under familiar settlement and clearance conditions.

(b) For the Issuer :

 (i) Raising capital.

(ii) Exposure in international market.

(iii) Enhances company's visibility, status and profile.

Difference between ADR and GDR :

- Both ADR and GDR are depository receipts, and represent an ownership of the underlying shares.
- The only difference is the location where they are traded.
- ADR's are traded in USA, whereas GDR's are traded in a country other than USA.

10. Global Debt Instruments (ECB, Eurobond, Foreign Bond) :

- These refer to debt instruments through which a corporate (or the Government) can raise funds outside its country of incorporation.
- Several financial instruments such as ECB (External Commercial Borrowings), Eurobonds such as Dimsum bonds, and foreign bonds such as Yankee bonds are used increasingly alongwith rise of globalization.

(a) ECB (External Commercial Borrowings) :

- RBI defines ECB as "commercial loans in the form of bank loans, buyer's credit, supplier's credit, securitized instruments (e.g. floating rate notes and fixed rate bonds, non-convertible, optionally convertible or partially convertible preference shares) availed of from non-resident lenders with a minimum average maturity of three years".
- Indian companies can borrow funds from sources outside India, such as a foreign bank, through ECBs.
- Bank Loans, Buyer's Credit, Supplier's Credit, Securitized instruments like floating rate notes and fixed rate bonds, Foreign Currency Convertible Bonds (FCCBs), Preference Shares (non-convertible or partially/optionally convertible), Foreign Currency Exchangeable Bonds (FCEBs) are all considered as ECB's.
- They are required to conform to RBI's ECB policy norms .
- ECB Policy norms define Automatic or Approval Route, Eligible Borrowers, Recognized Lenders, Amount & All-in cost, Average Maturity, End-use Stipulations.

- RBI regulates the ECB route very closely. Hence, Indian entities can borrow through ECB only after confirming to various parameters such as minimum maturity, as well as the permitted and non-permitted end-uses.
- ECB is allowed through both, Automatic and approval routes.
- Under the Automatic route, companies in businesses, such as hotel, hospitals and software, can access the international market for raising debt up to a limit.
- Special Economic Zones and non-government organizations engaged in micro finance activities are also allowed to access the ECB window.
- Companies or industries that can apply through the Automatic route can also take the approval route if they need to borrow more than the allowed limit under the automatic route.

Need for ECB :

- Developing economies require external assistance due to the shortage of capital within the country.
- The saving generated by the citizens and tax revenues collected by the government are too low compared to the funds requirement for the development of the infrastructure sector, the industry and various other developmental activities.
- Through ECB, they can raise large amount of financing at lower rates of interest as compared to obtaining finance in these developing economies, as ECB rates are linked to LIBOR, and if a company has a good credit rating, it will enjoy low interest rates.
- These country's exports are not sufficient to cover the large imports of machinery, components, and related services due to an adverse balance of payment position.
- The government of these countries therefore, normally, encourage the inflow of external funds into the country.

Drawbacks of ECBs :

(i) The borrower can be in trouble if the position is not hedged properly and his country's currency depreciates sharply which will lead to increase in the company's liability.

(ii) At the macro level, higher level of borrowing from overseas may push the currency to appreciate, which makes exports uncompetitive in an international market.

(iii) Access to overseas market and cheaper credit is advantageous for bigger companies that can borrow abroad. However, smaller companies have to deal with higher cost of capital in the domestic market.

(b) Eurobond :

- It is a bond which is issued in a currency other than the currency of the country or market in which it is issued.
- Eurobonds are usually underwritten by a bank syndicate and placed in countries other than the one in whose currency the bond is denominated.
- Issuers of Eurobond are Multinational corporations, Large domestic corporations, and International institutions.
- Eurobonds are normally bearer bonds.
- For example, A eurodollar bond is denominated in U.S. dollars and issued in Japan by a Chinese company .Here, the Chinese company could issue the eurodollar bond in any country other than the U.S.

Advantages of the Eurobonds :

For Investors :

(i) Interest can be paid free of income tax.

(ii) Issuers have high credit standing (government, international organisations or MNCs).

(iii) They are rated instruments.

(iv) Small par values.

(v) High liquidity.

For Issuers :

(i) They give issuers the flexibility to choose the country in which to offer their bond as per the country's regulatory constraints.

(ii) They can denominate their eurobond in their preferred currency.

(iii) Dimsum bond is one of the popular Eurobonds used over these years.

Dimsum Bond :

- This bond denominated in Chinese yuan and issued in Hong Kong.
- These bonds are issued outside China but denominated in Chinese renminbi/ yuan.
- It can be called as China's offshore renminbi bond market.
- China's domestic debt market is closed to foreign investors.

- So foreign investors can have an exposure on Chinese currency and its debt markets through Dimsum bonds
- The term Dimsum is derived from the Chinese cuisine that involves serving a variety of small delicacies and is very popular in Hong Kong.
- Deregulation led to the development of an offshore market in renminbi and the internationalization of Dimsum bonds.
- 131 billion yuan in Dimsum bonds were issued in the year 2011.

(c) Foreign Bond :

- A Foreign bond is issued in a domestic market by a foreign entity, in the domestic market's currency.
- Foreign firms carrying out a large amount of business in the domestic market, usually, issue foreign bonds.
- Foreign bonds are thus, sold outside borrower's country and are denominated by the currency of the country where issued.
- Foreign bonds are regulated by the domestic market authorities.
- They are usually given nicknames referring to the domestic market in which they are being offered.
- Examples of foreign bonds are Samurai bonds(Japanese Yen), Bulldog bonds (pounds) etc.
- Issuers issue foreign bonds with a desire to lower cost of capital.
- Investors find them attractive because they can add foreign securities to their portfolio, without being subjected to exchange rate exposure.

Categories/Forms of Foreign Bonds :

- Some foreign bonds are as given below:

(i) Yankee Bonds :

- Dollar-denominated bonds.
- Issued by Non-American borrowers in the U.S. market.

(ii) Samurai Bonds :

- Yen-denominated bonds.
- Issued by Non-Japanese borrowers in the Japanese market.

(iii) Bulldog Bonds :

- Pound sterling-denominated bonds.
- Issued by non-British borrowers in the British market.

(iv) Heidi Bonds :
- Franc-denominated bonds (Swiss franc is Swedish currency).
- Issued by Non-Swiss borrowers in the Swiss market.

(v) Rembrandt Bonds :
- Euro-denominated bonds (These bonds were earlier denominated in guilder, the Dutch currency at that time).
- Issued by non-Dutch borrowers in the Dutch market.

(vi) Matador Bonds :
- Euro-denominated bonds (These bonds were earlier denominated in peseta ,the Spanish currency at that time).
- Issued by non-Spanish borrowers in the Spanish market.

3.7 SECURITIES AND EXCHANGE BOARD OF INDIA (SEBI)- CAPITAL MARKETS REGULATOR/ROLE OF SEBI IN CAPITAL MARKET

Introduction :
- The Bombay Stock Exchange (BSE) and the National Stock Exchange of India Ltd (NSE) are the two primary exchanges in India.
- In addition, there are 23 Regional Stock Exchanges in India.
- These stock exchanges acquired a bad reputation due to illegal activities and frauds. Best known amongst them were the Harshad Mehta Scam and Ketan Parekh Scam.
- As a result, investors had lost a sense of trust when investing in equity shares of companies listed on the stock exchanges.
- In order to restore investor's confidence in stock markets and to regulate and monitor the activities of these stock exchanges, the need of a regulatory body became essential.
- To fulfill this requirement of investors, the Securities and Exchange Board of India (SEBI) was established by the Government of India in 1988 through an executive resolution.
- In addition, subsequently, it was upgraded as a fully autonomous body (a Statutory Board) in the year 1992 with the passing of the Securities and Exchange Board of India Act on 30th January, 1992.

- SEBI has four different departments namely, Primary department, Issue management and intermediaries department, Secondary department and Institutional investment department.
- After establishment of SEBI, the government gave statutory powers in 1992 through the Securities and Exchange Board of India (SEBI) Act. Now, SEBI has powers to seek information and records from banks and many other authorities, and for inspection of the books of accounts of listed companies.

Preamble :

The Preamble of the Securities and Exchange Board of India describes the basic functions of the Securities and Exchange Board of India as -

"...to protect the interests of investors in securities and to promote the development of and to regulate the securities market and for matters connected therewith or incidental thereto."

Objectives of SEBI:

- Securities and exchange board of India act, 1992 states the following objectives of SEBI:

1. To protect the interests of investors in securities.
2. To promote the development of and to regulate the securities market.
3. For matters connected therewith or incidental thereto

Purpose and Role of SEBI :

- SEBI was set-up with the main purpose of keeping a check on malpractices in security markets and protect the interest of investors.
- It was set-up with an intention to meet the needs of the following groups :

1. **Issuers :**
- For issuers, it provides a market place in which they can raise finance effectively and in a hassle free manner.

2. **Investors :**
- It provides investor protection and supplies them with accurate information.

3. **Intermediaries :**
- For intermediaries, it provides a competitive professional market.

Regulation of SEBI :

- In India, SEBI is a regulator for capital markets.

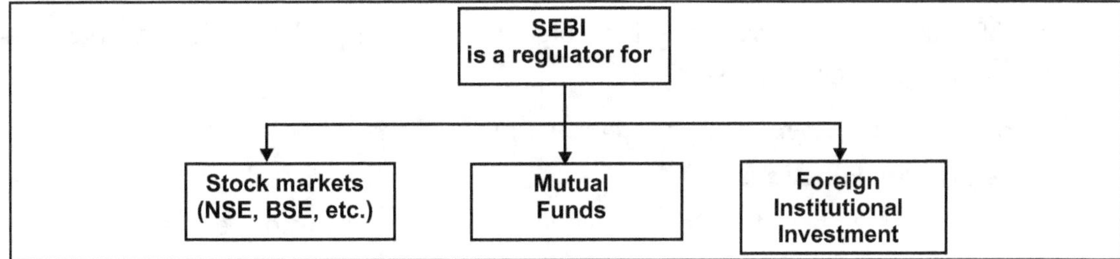

Fig. 3.4 : Regulation by SEBI

Functions of SEBI :

- Functions of SEBI can be classified as:

1. Protective Functions,

2. Developmental Functions,

3. Regulatory Functions.

1. Protective Functions :

- SEBI performs these functions in order to protect the interest of investor and provide safety of investment.

- Listed below are protective functions of SEBI:

(a) prohibiting fraudulent and unfair trade practices relating to securities markets.

(b) prohibiting insider trading in securities.

(c) keep a check on price manipulation and price rigging.

(d) SEBI imparts information and education to investors so that they can take sound decision when investing in securities market.

2. Developmental Functions :

- SEBI performs these functions to promote and develop activities in stock exchange and increase the business in stock exchange.

- Listed below are developmental functions of SEBI:

(a) training of intermediaries of securities markets.

(b) promoting investors' education.

(c) SEBI tries to promote activities of stock exchange by adopting a flexible approach.

(d) SEBI has permitted internet trading through registered stockbrokers.

(e) SEBI has made underwriting optional to reduce the cost of issue.

(f) Even initial public offer of primary market is permitted through stock exchange.

(g) SEBI publishes information and research works useful to all market participants.

(h) Promotion of fair practices.

(i) Promotion of self-regulatory organizations.

3. **Regulatory Functions :**

- SEBI performs these functions to regulate the business in stock exchange.

- Listed below are some regulatory functions of SEBI:

(a) Regulating the business in stock exchanges and any other securities markets.

(b) Registering and regulating the working of stock brokers, sub-brokers, share transfer agents, bankers to an issue, trustees of trust deeds, registrars to an issue, merchant bankers, underwriters, portfolio managers, investment advisers and such other intermediaries who may be associated with securities markets in any manner.

(c) Registering and regulating the working of the depositories, custodians of securities, foreign institutional investors, credit rating agencies and such other intermediaries as the Board may, by notification, specify in this behalf.

(d) Registering and regulating the working of venture capital funds and collective investment schemes including mutual funds.

(e) Regulating self-regulatory organizations.

(f) Regulating substantial acquisition of shares and takeover of companies.

(g) Calling for information from, undertaking inspection, conducting inquiries and audits of the stock exchanges, mutual funds, other persons associated with the securities market, intermediaries and self-regulatory organizations in the securities market.

Powers of SEBI :

- In 1995, SEBI was given additional statutory power by the Government of India through an amendment to the Securities and Exchange Board of India Act, 1992.

Powers of SEBI include :

1. Inspect the books of accounts from recognized stock exchanges.

2. Inspect the books of accounts of financial intermediaries.

3. Call for periodical returns from recognized stock exchanges.

4. To call information or explanation from recognized stock exchanges or their members.

5. Direct enquiries in relation to affairs of stock exchanges or their members.

6. To grant approval to byelaws of recognized stock exchanges.

7. Power to regulate malpractices in security markets such as insider trading, price rigging and punish the offenders thereof.

8. To grant registration to market intermediaries such as brokers etc.

9. Control and regulate stock exchanges.

10. Suspend stock markets operation.

11. SEBI has the authority to impose monetary penalties on capital market intermediaries and other participants for a range of violations. It can even order for suspension of their registration for a short period.

12. Order investigation of participants in capital markets.

Questions for Discussion :

1. What is Capital market? Explain its components.

2. Explain the importance of Capital market.

3. Distinguish between Primary markets and Secondary markets.

4. Explain the Role of SEBI as a Capital Market Regulator.

5. Explain Bonds and Debentures as Capital market instruments.

6. Explain the various Global Debt Instruments used in Capital markets.

7. Explain the detailed Process of IPO .

8. Write Short Notes on:

(A) Preference Shares.

(B) Equity Shares.

(C) Non-voting Shares.

(D) Compulsory Convertible Debentures (CCD).

(E) Fixed Deposits.

(F) Debentures .

(G) Bonds.

(H) Global Depository receipts.

(I)   American Depository receipts.

(J)   Global Debt Instruments.

(K)   Eurobond.

(L)   Primary Market.

(M)   Secondary Market.

(N)   Eurobond.

(O)   ECB.

(P)   Foreign Bond.

(Q)   SEBI.

(R)   IPO.

(S)   BSE.

(T)   NSE.

(U)   Stock Exchange.

Chapter **4**...

Banks and NBFCs

Contents ...

Learning Objectives...

After studying this chapter, the student should understand:

- **Different types of Banks :** Central Bank, Nationalized & Co Operative Banks, Regional Rural Banks, Scheduled Banks, Private Banks & Foreign Banks, Mudra Bank, Specialized Banks.

- Concept of NBFC and different types of NBFC's.

- Different types of Banking : Wholesale Banking, Retail Banking, Investment Banking, Corporate Banking, Private Banking, Development Banking.

4.1 INTRODUCTION TO BANK

- The term bank is derived from a French word 'banque', meaning a bench or money exchange table.
- In India, banking is as old as ancient Vedic times.
- There were bankers known as Sheth, Shah carried out the functions of banking.
- Bank is a place where citizens of a country can place their hard-earned money (deposits) in a safe and secured manner and in addition, earn an interest on this money.
- In addition, banks provide an avenue for businesses and individuals to get money/ credit/ finance that they require for various purposes.
- A bank is a financial intermediary, which accepts deposits from surplus areas and loans out these funds to deficit areas.
- For example, a salaried person will have certain savings, after satisfying his daily needs, and businesses may require finance for their expansion and modernization activities. The bank here will accept deposits from these salaried people and lend this money to business house.
- In most countries in the world, either the government or a central bank regulates banking sector.
- For example, Reserve bank of India (RBI), the central bank of the country regulates all commercial banks. Popular banks in India are SBI (State Bank of India), BOB (Bank of Baroda), ICICI, HDFC and many others.

Definition :

> *"A Banking Company means any company, which transacts the business of banking in India. Here, 'banking' means accepting, for the purpose of lending or investment, of deposits of money from the public, repayable on demand or otherwise, and withdrawable by cheque, draft, and order or otherwise."*
>
> *— **Banking Regulation Act, 1949***

- We can simply define Bank as a financial institution that undertakes the banking activity. It accepts deposits and then lends the same to earn a profit

- Thus, a bank is a financial institution, which accepts deposits and lends to prospective borrowers to withdraw and transfer their money from accounts through cheque or electronic banking transactions.

4.2 CLASSIFICATION AND TYPES OF BANKS

Classification of Banks

Commercial Banks

- For profit motive
- Business orientation professionalism

Regional Rural Banks

- Hybrid between commercial and co-operative banks
- Formed to combine best features of both commercial and co-operative

Co-operative Banks

- No profit, no loss basis.
- Oriented towards rural areas, weaker sections, agriculture and small businesses.

Fig. 4.1 : Classification of Banks

- Banks in India are classified mainly into two types:
1. Commercial banks.
2. Co-operative banks.
3. Regional Rural Banks (RRBs) can be added.

4.3 COMMERCIAL BANKS

- Commercial means that these banks operate 'for profit'.
- Profit is the main motive behind the existence of these banks.
- A group of individuals owns these banks.
- Commercial banks deal with the deposits and loans of businesses and individuals,
- Banks issue bank cheques and drafts, as well as accept money on term deposits (FD).
- Commercial banks also play the role of moneylenders, via installment loans and overdrafts.
- Commercial banks provide a variety of deposit accounts, such as savings and time deposit.

Classification of Commercial banks :

- Commercial banks are further classified into four types:
1. Public Sector Banks /Nationalised banks,
2. Private Sector Banks,
3. Foreign Banks,
4. Differential Banks.

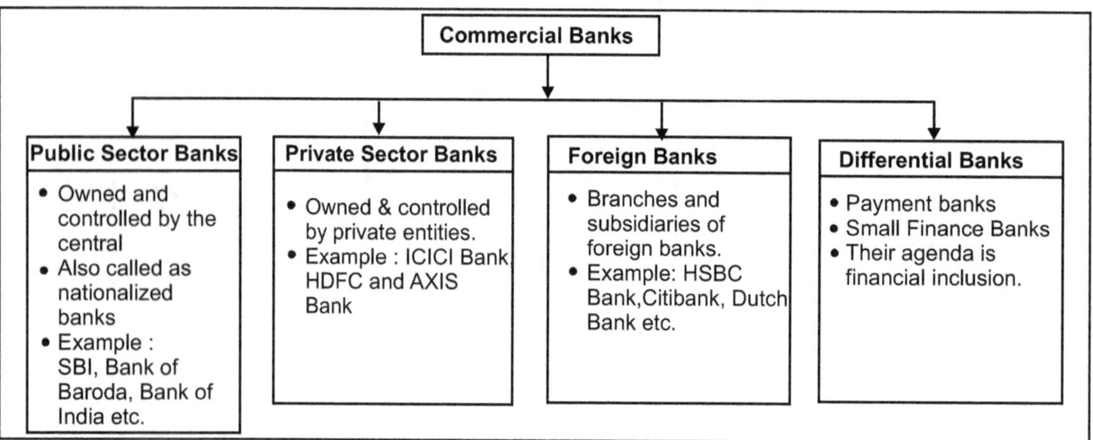

Fig. 4.2 : Classification of Commercial Banks

(1) Public Sector Banks/Nationalised Banks :

- In public sector banks, the Government controls a majority shareholdings.
- In all these banks, Government's share is more than 51 %.
- In other words, Government of India (GOI) is the promoter of these banks.
- Apart from profit motive, these banks also have the mandate to fulfill Government's social and developmental goals.
- Public sector banks include 19 nationalised banks and IDBI Bank.
- Today, public sector banks account for nearly 70 % of the total banking business in India.
- State Bank of India (SBI) is the largest commercial bank in terms of business volume.

(2) Private Sector Banks :

- In private sector banks in India, major stake or equity are held by the private individuals and not by government.
- These banks are registered as companies with limited liability.
- In India, private sector banks include ICICI Banks, HDFC Bank, Axis Bank etc.

(3) Foreign Banks :

- When one refers to foreign banks, it means that the bank has its head office located in the foreign country and is operating in India through its branches or subsidiaries.
- Foreign banks operating in India include Citibank, HSBC, and Standard Chartered etc.
- A foreign bank has to follow the regulations of both its home country and the host country.
- The number of foreign banks has increased considerably in India since he economic reforms of 1991.
- Foreign banks perform important functions such as providing assistance for exports, foreign currency transactions, Issuing letter of credit etc.

(4) Differential Banks :

- Differential banks are different from other commercial banks in terms of the following areas:

(a) are formed for a particular segment of consumers or a particular purpose.

(b) restricted in its geographical reach.

(c) restricted in banking operations(deposit and lending operations).

- Two important differential banks in India are:

(a) Payments banks,

(b) Small finance banks.

(a) Payments Banks :

- Payments bank is a new model of banks conceptualised by the Reserve Bank of India (RBI).
- The objective behind Payments banks is to strengthen the Government's objective of financial inclusion and help expand banking services.
- These banks are targeted towards people without access to the formal banking system, such as migrant workers, low-income households and small businesses.
- These banks are intended to provide savings, deposit, and payment and remittance services to these sections.
- These banks are not allowed to be in the business of lending.

Features of Payment Banks :

(i) Accept a restricted deposit (currently limit is to ₹ 1 lakh per customer).

(ii)   These banks cannot issue loans or credit cards.

(iii)   Payments bank can offer the facilities of current and savings accounts, and issue ATM and debit cards. They can also offer net-banking and mobile-banking services for customer ease.

- In 2015, Reserve Bank of India (RBI) gave in-principle approval to 11 entities to open 'payment banks'.

    Payment Banks : The list of 11 entities is as below :

- Aditya Birla Nuvo Ltd.
- Airtel M Commerce Services Ltd.
- Cholamandalam Distributions Ltd.
- Reliance Industries Ltd.
- Tech Mahindra Ltd.
- Vodafone m-Pesa Ltd.
- Fino Pay Tech Ltd.
- Department of Posts.
- National Securities Depository Ltd (NSDL).
- Dilip Shanghavi (founder of Sun Pharmaceutical Industries Ltd).
- Vijay Shekhar Sharma, founder of One97 Communications Ltd that runs mobile payment company Pay TM.

(b)   Small Finance Banks :

- Small finance banks are meant for financial inclusion.
- A small finance bank is a niche type of bank targeted towards people who traditionally have not used banks.

Regulations for Small Finance Banks :

(i)   Open at least 25% of its branches in unbanked regions (areas that do not have any other bank branches).

(ii)   It should hold 75% of its net credits in loans to firms in priority sector lending, and 50% of the loans in its portfolio must be less than ₹ 25 lakh.

(iii)   In 2016,RBI granted approval and necessary licenses to ten entities to set-up small finance banks.

4.4 CO-OPERATIVE BANKS

* As the name suggests, co-operative bank is set-up on the principles of mutual help and co-operation.

* Co-operative banks belongs to its members, who are simultaneously the owners as well as the customers of the bank.

* Intended to provide rural credit, co-operative banks are created by persons belonging to the same local or professional community or sharing a common interest.

* Members from a community band together to extend loans to each other at favourable terms.

* In other words, when a co-operative society engages itself in banking business, it is called a Co-operative Bank.

* The history of Indian Co-operative Banking can be traced to passing of Co-operative Societies Act, 1904,whose objective was to establish co-operative credit societies "to encourage thrift, self-help and co-operation among agriculturists, artisans and persons of limited means."

* Co-operative banks operate on a "No-profit, No-loss" principle.

* Co-operative banks provide a wide range of banking and financial services such as loans, deposits, banking accounts etc. to their members.

* The banking products offered by co-operative banks are limited.

* These banks are specialists in agriculture-related products and generally finance agricultural activities, small-scale industries and self-employed workers.

* The first co-operative bank in India was Anyonya Sahakari Mandali, established in 1889 in the province of Baroda.

* In India, co-operative banks are broadly classified into urban co-operative banks and rural co-operative banks, depending on their region of operation.

Three tier structures exist in the Co-operative banking (short-term) as below:

* State Co-operative Bank (which operate at the apex level in states),

* District Central Co-operative Banks (operate at the district level),

* Primary Agricultural Credit Societies (operate at the village or grass-root level).

Long-term Structure of Co-operative Banks :

- State Co-operative Agriculture and Rural Development Banks (SCARDS) operating at the state-level.

- Primary Co-operative Agriculture and Rural Development Banks (PCARDBS), operating at district/block level.

Difference between Commercial Bank and Co-operative Bank :

Basis	Commercial bank	Co-operative bank
1. Principle :	For-profit.	No profit, no loss principle; service motive.
2. Area of Operation :	Countrywide operations.	Operations restricted to a specific area.
3. Voting Power :	Decided by the number of shares purchased.	One member, one vote.
4. Scope of Services :	All banking services.	Are restricted to agricultural and rural credit; small scale industries.
5. Borrowers :	Accountholders of banks.	Members/ shareholders.
6. Interest Rates on Deposits :	Lesser than Co-operative banks.	Slightly higher than Commercial Banks.
7. Related Acts :	Banking Regulations Act, 1949.	Cooperative Credit Societies Act, 1904.
8. Regulators :	RBI only.	Dual regulation i.e., Registrar of Co-operative Societies and RBI (partially).

4.5 REGIONAL RURAL BANK (RRB)

- It was found that Commercial banks had the expertise and professionalism. However, they were not much oriented towards socio-economic developmental goals of the Government and did not disburse much credit to rural areas, agriculturists, weaker sections and small-scale industries.

- On the other hand, co-operative banks disbursed credit to rural areas and small-scale industries, but they lacked the expertise and professionalism.

- Therefore, the Government decided to create a hybrid of these two (commercial banks and co-operative banks), which will have the best features of both.
- Therefore, this new entity (RRB) will have orientation towards rural areas and participate in socio-economic development goals of the Government.
- At the same time, they will have the banking expertise, professional management and business orientation.
- Thus was the concept of these new entities, RRB (Regional Rural banks).
- Government of India (GOI) set-up Regional Rural Banks (RRBs) on 2nd October, 1975 with an objective to provide credit to the weaker sections of the rural areas, particularly the small and marginal farmers, agricultural labourers, and small entrepreneurs.
- RRBs were set-up as government-sponsored, regional based rural lending institutions under the Regional Rural Banks Act, 1976.

   Ownership Pattern of RRB :
- RRB has a sponsor bank, which is a public sector bank.
- For instance, SBI is a sponsor bank for 14 RRBs.
- Apart from that, Central Government and State Government also sponsor RRB.
- Shareholding percentage/ Ownership pattern among central government, sponsor bank and state government is given in the table below:

Central Government	State Government	Sponsor Bank
50 %	15 %	35 %

4.6 SCHEDULED AND NON-SCHEDULED BANKS

- The scheduled banks are the ones, which are enshrined, in the second schedule of the RBI Act, 1934.
- All commercial banks in India, i.e.; public sector, private sector and foreign banks, regional rural banks, and state cooperative banks are scheduled banks.

   They meet the following two criteria :
- Paid-up capital and reserves of an aggregate value of not less than ₹ 5 lakhs.
- Satisfy RBI that their affairs are carried out in the interest of their depositors.
- Scheduled banks have to fulfill certain obligations like maintenance of reserves (CRR, SLR etc).
- In return, they can approach RBI for financial assistance, refinance etc.

- Non- scheduled banks are those banks which are not included in the Second schedule of the RBI Act, 1934.
- At present these are only three such banks in the country.
- Unlike scheduled banks, they are not entitled to borrow from the RBI for normal banking purposes, except in emergency or "abnormal circumstances.

4.7 SPECIALIZED BANKS

- There are three important specialized banks with different functions, viz.;
1. Export Import Bank of India (EXIM Bank),
2. Small Industries Development Bank of India (SIDBI),
3. National Bank for Agriculture and Rural Development (NABARD).

1. EXIM Bank :

- Export-Import Bank of India is the premier export finance institution of the country.
- It commenced operations in 1982 under the Export-Import Bank of India Act, 1981.
- Government of India launched the institution with a mandate to not just enhance exports from India, but also to integrate the country's foreign trade and investment with the overall economic growth.
- Exim Bank of India has been both a catalyst and a key player in the promotion of cross border trade and investment.
- Commencing operations as a purveyor of export credit, like other Export Credit Agencies in the world, Exim Bank of India has evolved into an institution that plays a major role in partnering Indian industries, particularly the Small and Medium Enterprises through a wide range of products and services offered at all stages of the business cycle, starting from import of technology and export product development to export production, export marketing, pre-shipment and post-shipment and overseas investment.

Objective :

"For providing financial assistance to exporters and importers, and for functioning as the principal financial institution for coordinating the working of institutions engaged in financing export and import of goods and services with a view to promoting the country's international trade..."

(The Export-Import Bank of India Act, 1981)

Functions :

- EXIM as a specialized bank thus, has two broad functions:

(a) Financial services, which includes loans to Exporters and Importers, Commercial banks, Foreign governments through its products such as Buyer's credit, Supplier's credit, Line of credit, Pre-shipment finance, Post-shipment finance, Guarantees, Refinance of export credit etc.

(b) Provides information about the international market, including guidance about the opportunities for export or import, the risks involved in it and the competition to be faced, and the like through its research and advisory wings.

2. Small Industries Development Bank of India (SIDBI) :

- Small Industries Development Bank of India (SIDBI) set-up on 2nd April, 1990 under an Act of Indian Parliament.

- SIDBI acts as the Principal Financial Institution for Promotion, Financing and Development of the Micro, Small and Medium Enterprise (MSME) sector as well as for co-ordination of functions of institutions engaged in similar activities.

- As a Principal Financial Institution for MSMEs, SIDBI has dedicated its resources towards evolution of a vibrant MSME eco-system.

- SIDBI's initiatives have remained aligned to the national goals of poverty alleviation, employment generation, promoting entrepreneurship and fostering competitiveness in MSME sector.

- As a specialized bank, SIDBI grants loans to those individuals who want to establish a small-scale business unit.

- SIDBI started as a development bank, exclusively for the small scale industries.

- The main objective of SIDBI is to promote and develop small industries by providing them the much needed production finance.

- SIDBI also co-ordinates the working of institutions and commercial banks which supply finance (long-term and short-term) to small entrepreneurs.

Mission :

- To facilitate and strengthen credit flow to MSMEs and address both financial and developmental gaps in the MSME eco-system.

Functions :

- SIDBI carries the following important functions:

(a) SIDBI promotes employment oriented industries to create more employment opportunities.

(b) SIDBI supports MSME for technology adoption and upgradation , as well as modernisation of existing units. It also helps to enlarge marketing capabilities of small industries.

(c) SIDBI participates in the equity type of loans on soft terms, term loan, working capital (both in rupee and foreign currencies), venture capital support, and different forms of resource support to banks and other institutions.

(d) SIDBI facilitates timely flow of credit (both long-term loans and short-term-cash credit) for working capital to MSME's in collaboration with commercial banks.

(e) SIDBI discounts and re-discounts bills with a view to encourage bills culture , and help small enterprises to realise their sale proceeds in a smooth, hassle free manner .

3.   National Bank for Agriculture and Rural Development (NABARD) :

- It was established on 12 July, 1982 by a special act by the Parliament.
- This specialized bank is a central institution for financing agricultural and rural sectors.
- It provides short-term and long-term credit through Regional Rural Banks.
- It provides financial assistance for agricultural purposes, poultry farming, small-scale industries, cottage industries, handicrafts, weaving, fishing, and allied economic activities in rural areas.
- NABARD basically undertakes measures towards institution building for improving absorptive capacity of the credit delivery system, which includes:

(a) Formulation of rehabilitation schemes,

(b) Monitoring of rehabilitation schemes,

(c) Restructuring of credit institutions,

(d) Training of personnel.

Major Functions :

(a) NABARD refinances the financial institutions which finances the rural sector.

(b) NABARD helps to develop institutions which assist the rural economy.

(c) NABARD co-ordinates the rural financing activities of all institutions engaged in developmental work at the field level. It maintains liaison with the Central

Government, State Government, Reserve Bank of India (RBI) and other National level Institutions concerned with policy formulation.

(d) NABARD undertakes monitoring and evaluation of its refinanced projects.

(e) NABARD keeps a check on its client institutes.

(f) NABARD regulates the institutions which provide financial assistance to the rural economy. Even Co-operative banks and the RRB are regulated by NABARD.

(g) NABARD provides training facilities to the institutions working for the upliftment of rural areas.

4.8 MUDRA (MICRO UNITS DEVELOPMENT AND REFINANCE AGENCY

- Micro Units Development and Refinance Agency (MUDRA) was incorporated as a NBFC in order to "fund the unfunded", bring such enterprise in to the formal financial system, and support development of micro enterprise sector.
- This scheme was launched in April 2015, and its objective is to refinance collateral-free loans given by the lenders to small borrowers.
- It enables small borrowers to borrow from all financial institutions such as Public Sector Banks (PSBs), Regional Rural and Co-operative banks, Private Sector Banks, Foreign Banks, Micro Finance Institutions and Non-Banking Finance Companies.
- Under the scheme, loans are given to non-farm income generating enterprises in manufacturing and trading and services whose credit needs are below ₹10 lakh.
- PMMY can be availed under three categories:
1. Shishu, which will cover loans up to ₹ 50,000;
2. Kishor for loans above ₹ 50,000 and up to ₹ 5 lakh;
3. Tarun for loans above ₹ 5 lakh and up to ₹ 10 lakh.
- Government would ensure that 60% of the funds under this scheme would flow to Shishu category and the rest to Kishor and Tarun categories.
- Due to this scheme, the government has ensured credit flow to the SME sector and recognized that NBFCs are a good fit to reach out to them.
- MUDRA Debit Cards are the unique feature of this scheme. Using these cards, people can withdraw money in order to provide for their working capital needs through ATMs.
- This scheme would enable SMEs to get refinance at subsidized rates and thereby expand their activities.

4.9 CENTRAL BANK

- Central bank refers to a country's apex financial institution, and the nation's independent monetary authority.
- Being an apex bank, central bank regulates other banks in the system.
- As the Central bank is monetary authority, it formulates monetary policy to control money supply in the country.
- In other words, control over the production and distribution of money and credit for a nation.

Definitions:

1. **Samuelson :** *"Every Central Bank has one function. It operates to control economy, supply of money and credit."*
2. **Vera Smith :** *"The primary definition of Central Bank is the banking system in which a single bank has either a complete or residuary monopoly of note issue."*
3. **Kent :** *"Central Bank may be defined as an institution which is charged with the responsibility of managing the expansion and contraction of the volume of money in the interest of general public welfare."*

- Every country has its own Central bank to manage the money supply and the banking and financial system in the country.
- India's Central Bank is Reserve Bank of India(RBI),fully owned by the Government of India.
- RBI regulates the issue of Bank notes and keeping of reserves with a view to securing monetary stability in India and operates the currency and credit system of the country to its advantage.
- RBI has a modern monetary policy framework to meet the challenge of an increasingly complex economy, to maintain price stability while keeping in mind the objective of growth.

Functions of RBI (Central Bank) :

1. **Formulation of Monetary and Credit Policy :**
- Monetary policy refers to the use of monetary instruments under the control of the central bank to influence variables and regulate various aspects of monetary policy such as interest rates, money supply and availability of credit with a view to achieving the ultimate objective of economic policy.

- It is a policy by which desired level of money flow and its demand is regulated in the economy.
- Central bank use monetary policy to achieve economic stability.
- In India, RBI formulates, implements, and monitors the monetary policy.
- The objective of monetary policy is maintaining price stability while keeping in mind the objective of growth.
- Apart from maintaining price stability, ensuring adequate flow of credit in the productive sectors of the economy and maintaining orderly conditions in the financial markets emerged as an additional objective in the aftermath of liberalization and globalization.
- Thus, over time the role of monetary and credit policy evolved to maintain a judicious balance between price stability, economic growth and financial stability.

2. **Regulator and Supervisor of the Financial System :**
- Well-functioning, liquid and resilient financial markets help monetary policy transmission as well as in allocation and absorption of risks entailed in financing India's growth.
- As a regulator of financial system in the country, RBI prescribes broad parameters of banking operations within which country's banking and financial system functions.
- Objective of this function is to maintain public confidence in the system, protect depositors' interest and provide cost-effective banking services to the public.
- RBI is a regulator for the following financial entities/markets:
(a) Money market,
(b) Foreign exchange market,
(c) Commercial banks,
(d) Co-operative banks (duality of control over these banks with banking related functions being regulated by the Reserve Bank of India and management related functions regulated by respective State Governments/Central Government.)
(e) NBFC's.

3. **Manager of Foreign Exchange :**
- RBI manages and administers the Foreign Exchange Management Act (FEMA), 1999.

- It manages foreign exchange with an objective to facilitate external trade and payment and promote orderly development and maintenance of foreign exchange market in India.
- RBI stabilizes the exchange rate of rupee, and is a guardian/ keeper of the foreign currency reserves of the country.

4.   Issuer of Currency :

- RBI issues and exchanges or destroys currency and coins not fit for circulation.
- It is an issuing agency of the currency and coins other than rupee one currency and coin which are issued by Ministry of Finance.
- RBI is responsible to supply to the public, adequate quantity of supplies of currency notes and coins, and in good quality.

5.   Developmental Role :

- RBI performs a wide range of promotional and developmental functions to support national objectives.
- Under this role, it did set-up institutions like IDBI, NABARD, SIDBI, NHB etc.

6.   Banker and Debt Manager to the Government :

- RBI performs merchant banking function for the central and the state governments and also acts as their banker.

7.   Banker to Banks :

- RBI maintains banking accounts of all scheduled banks. Even banks need their own mechanism to transfer funds and settle inter-bank transaction such as borrowing from and lending to other banks and customer transactions. As the banker to banks, the RBI fulfills this role.
- In this role, RBI performs following tasks:
(a) Enables smooth, swift and seamless clearing and settlement of inter-bank transactions.
(b) Provide an efficient means of funds transfer for banks.
(c) Enable banks to maintain their accounts with the Reserve Bank for statutory reserve requirements and maintenance of transaction balances.
(d) Acting as a lender of last resort, wherein RBI comes to the rescue of a bank that is solvent but faces temporary liquidity problems by supplying it with much needed liquidity when no one else is willing to extend credit to that bank.

8. **Consumer Education and Protection :**
- The Reserve Bank's approach to customer service focusses on protection of customers' rights, enhancing the quality of customer service, spreading awareness and strengthening the grievance redressal mechanism in the banks and in the RBI.

9. **Financial Inclusion and Development :**
- Financial inclusion may be defined as the process of ensuring access to financial services and timely and adequate credit where needed by vulnerable groups such as weaker sections and low-income groups at an affordable cost.
- Financial Inclusion and Financial Literacy are considered as twin pillars where Financial Inclusion acts on the supply side i.e. for creating access and Financial Literacy acts from the demand side i.e. creating a demand for the financial products and services.
- Consumer protection is considered the third pillar of sustainable and inclusive financial growth.
- This role encapsulates the essence of renewed national focus on financial inclusion, promoting financial education and literacy and making credit available to productive sectors of the economy including the rural and MSME sector and to the Priority sector.

   Monetary Policy and Tools :
- Being a central bank of the country, RBI formulates monetary policy bi-monthly (once in 2 months).
- Through the monetary policy, RBI regulates the cost & supply of money & credit in order to achieve the socio-economic objectives of the economy.
- Money supply is influenced through monetary policy.
- With increase in money supply, liquidity is enhanced in the system and vice-versa.
- RBI basically has three kinds of monetary policy tools to achieve its goals.
- These include :

1. **Setting of Reserve Requirements :**
- These refers to CRR (Cash Reserve ratio), wherein banks need to keep a proportion of their deposits, which in turn affects the lending capacity of the banks.

2. **Use of Open Market Operations (OMO) :**
- RBI buys and sells securities from member banks.

3. **Set Targets on Interest Rates :**

- RBI influences interest rates in the economy through Repo rate, which refers to the interest rate at which the banks borrow from RBI for short-term.

4.10 CONCEPT OF NBFC

- NBFCs are almost similar in its functions to a bank, but the main difference is that it does not allow its depositors to withdraw money from their accounts.
- As per RBI,
- NBFC is a company registered under the Companies Act, 2013 engaged in the business of loans and advances, acquisition of shares/ stocks/ bonds/ debentures/ securities issued by Government or local authority or other marketable securities of a like nature, leasing, hire-purchase, insurance business, chit business.
- However, NBFC does not include any institution whose principal business is that of agriculture activity, industrial activity, purchase or sale of any goods (other than securities) or providing any services and sale/purchase/construction of immovable property.
- A non-banking institution which is a company and has principal business of receiving deposits under any scheme or arrangement in one lumpsum or in installments by way of contributions or in any other manner, is also a NBFC

Non-banking → An entity which is not a bank.
Financial company → Deals in Loan and Financial products.

Difference between NBFC and Bank:

Basis	Bank	NBFC
1. **Deposits :**	Banks can accept all types of Deposit.	NBFC can accept only Term deposits. They cannot accept Demand deposits.
2. **Facility of Deposit Insurance by DICGC :**	Available for Banks.	Not available for NBFC.
3. **Cheque Facility :**	Banks can issue Cheques.	NBFC cannot issue Cheques.
4. **Incorporation :**	Banking Regulation Act, 1949.	Companies Act 1956.

Basis	Bank	NBFC
5. **Interest Rates for Advances/ Loans :**	Based on MCLR.	Depends on the risk factor.
6. **Maintenance of Reserve Ratios (CRR,SLR) :**	Compulsory.	Not required.
7. **Payment and Settlement Cycle :**	Banks are an integral part.	NBFCs are not a part.

4.11 CLASSIFICATION AND TYPES OF NBFCs

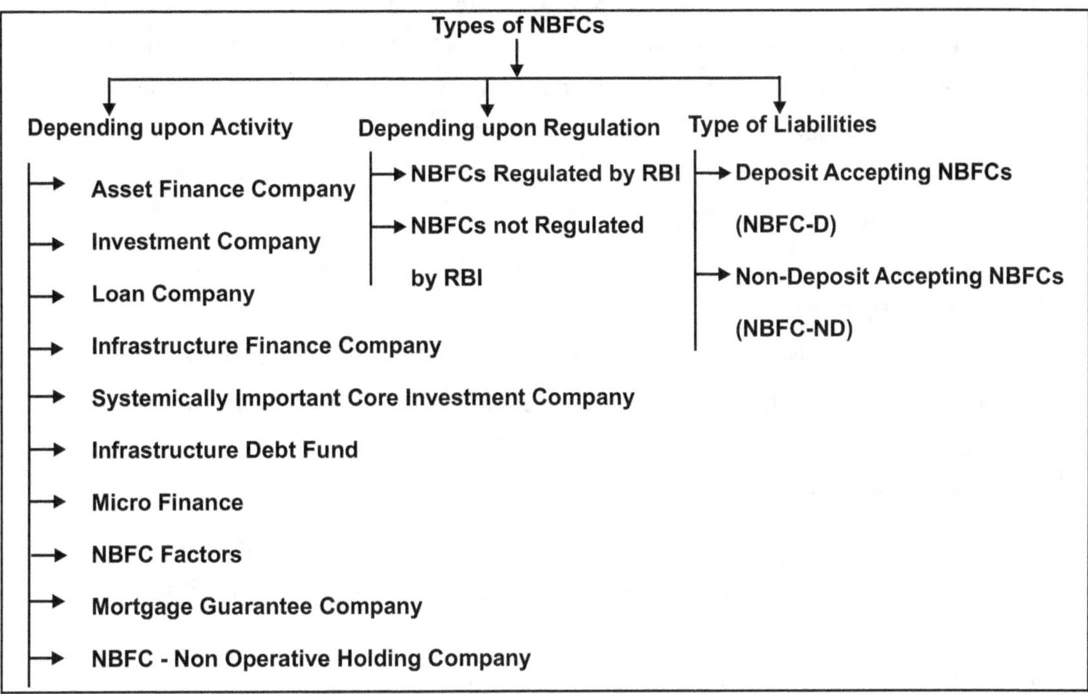

Fig. 4.3 : Types of NBFCs

(I)   In terms of the Type of Liabilities :

- Depending upon whether the NBFC can take deposits, it is classifies as Deposit and Non-Deposit accepting NBFC.

1.   Deposit Accepting NBFC (NBFC-D) :

- These NBFC's can accept deposits.

2.   Non- Deposit Accepting NBFC (NBFC-ND) :
- These NBFC's cannot accept deposits.
- These are further classified as NBFCs by their size into systemically important (NBFC-NDSI)and other non-deposit holding companies(NBFC-ND).
- NBFCs having asset size is of ₹ 500 cr or more are considered as systemically important NBFC's as their will have a bearing on the financial stability of the overall economy.

(II)   Depending upon the Kind of Activity :
- Here are several financial institutions which are classified, depending upon their principal business activities.

1.   Asset Finance Company (AFC) :
- Principal business of AFC include the financing of physical assets supporting productive/ economic activity, such as automobiles, tractors, lathe machines, generator sets, earth moving and material handling equipments, moving on own power and general purpose industrial machines.
- Income from its principal business is more than 60% of its total income for AFC.

2.   Investment Company (IC) :
- The principal business of IC is the acquisition of securities.

3.   Loan Company (LC) :
- Principal business of LC is the providing of finance (by making loans or advances or otherwise) for any activity other than its own , but does not include an Asset Finance Company.

4.   Infrastructure Finance Company (IFC) :
- IFC deploys at least 75 per cent of its total assets in infrastructure loans, has a minimum Net Owned Funds of ₹ 300 crore, and a minimum credit rating of 'A 'or equivalent.
- Additionally, IFC also needs to maintain a CRAR of 15%.

5.   Systemically Important Core Investment Company (CIC-ND-SI) :
- It is in the business of acquisition of shares and securities .
- CIC-ND-SI satisfies the following conditions:-
(a)   It holds more than 90% of its total assets in the form of investment in equity shares, preference shares, debt or loans in group companies;
(b)   Has an asset size of more than 100 crore rupees.

6. **Infrastructure Debt Fund - Non- Banking Financial Company (IDF-NBFC) :**
   - This type of NBFC is meant to facilitate the flow of long-term debt into infrastructure projects.
   - IDF-NBFC raise resources through issue of Rupee or Dollar denominated bonds of minimum 5 year maturity.
   - Only Infrastructure Finance Companies (IFC) can sponsor IDF-NBFCs.

7. **Non-Banking Financial Company - Micro Finance Institution (NBFC-MFI) :**
   - It is a non-deposit taking NBFC, having atleast 85% of its assets in the form of microfinance.

   Loan Criteria :
   - Microfinance loans should satisfy the following criteria:

   (a) Loan given to those who have annual income of ₹ 60,000 in rural areas and ₹ 1,20,000 in urban areas.

   (b) Such loans should not exceed ₹ 50,000 and its tenure should not be less than 24 months.

   (c) The loan has to be given without collateral.

   (d) Loan repayment is done on weekly, fortnightly or monthly installments at the choice of the borrower.

8. **Non-Banking Financial Company – Factors (NBFC-Factors) :**
   - It is a non-deposit taking NBFC engaged in the principal business of factoring.
   - The financial assets in the factoring business should constitute at least 50 percent of its total assets and its income derived from factoring business should not be less than 50 percent of its gross income.

9. **Mortgage Guarantee Companies (MGC) :**
   - These NBFC satisfy the following criteria:

   (a) They have more than 90% of the business turnover in mortgage guarantee business,

   (b) They have more than 90% of the gross income is from mortgage guarantee business, and

   (c) Net owned fund is ₹ 100 crore.

10. NBFC- Non-Operative Financial Holding Company (NOFHC) :

- It is financial institution through which promoter / promoter groups will be permitted to set-up a new bank.
- It's a wholly-owned Non-Operative Financial Holding Company (NOFHC) which will hold the bank as well as all other financial services companies regulated by RBI or other financial sector regulators, to the extent permissible under the applicable regulatory prescriptions.

(III) Depending upon the Regulators :

- Majority of the NBFC' are regulated by RBI.
- NBFC's are divided into :

1. NBFC's Regulated by RBI :

- RBI regulates the companies which deal in lending, accepting deposits, financial leasing, hire purchase and acquisition of shares / stocks etc.

2. NBFC's Not Regulated by RBI :

- These NBFC' have a regulator other than RBI.
- The table contains its list :

	NBFC	**Regulator**
1.	Stock broking and merchant banking companies.	SEBI.
2.	Nidhi Companies.	Ministry of Corporate Affairs, Government of India.
3.	Chit Funds.	State Governments.
4.	Insurance Companies.	IRDA.
5.	Housing Finance Companies.	NHB(National Housing Bank).

4.12 DIFFERENT TYPES OF BANKING

- Banking business can be divided into different types, based upon a number of criteria, such as:
- (i) Objectives,
- (ii) Clientele served,
- (iii) Services offered.

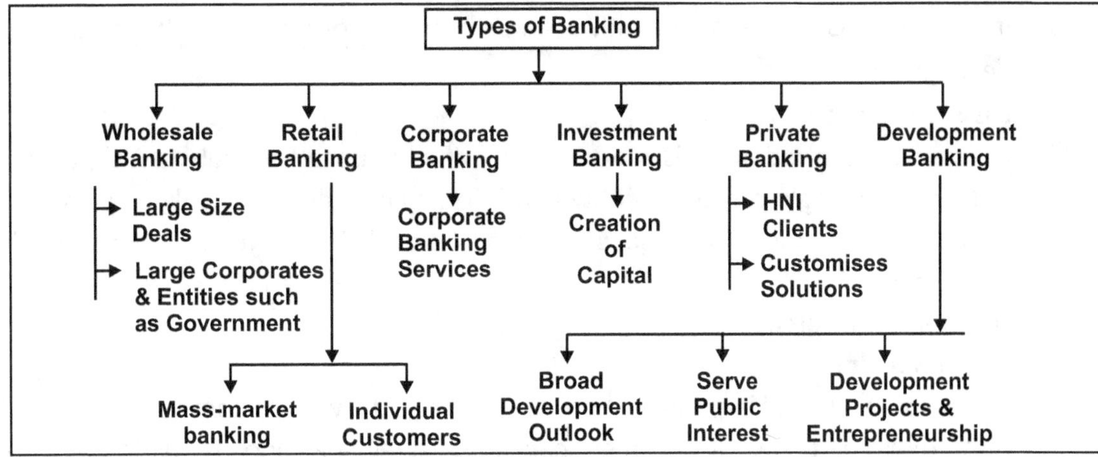

Fig. 4.4 : Types of Banking

1. Wholesale Banking :

- Wholesale banking refers to the financial practice of lending and borrowing between two large institutions.

- Wholesale services in bank are reserved only for government agencies, and high net-worth clients like corporates with strong financials, commercial banks, mid-size companies, pension funds, and other institutional customers of comparable size and stature.

- These services are made up of cash management, equipment financing, large loans, merchant banking, and trust services, among others.

- In case of wholesale banking, deals of large amounts take place , as a result of which large organizations or institutions are offered special prices or reduced fees, for banking services.

Services of Wholesale Banking :

(a) Working capital financing,

(b) Mergers and Acquisitions,

(c) Fund management,

(d) Underwriting,

(e) Term loans for Corporates,

(f) Large trade transactions,

(g) Currency conversion.

Advantages :

(a) Large deals can help in reduction in service costs.

(b) It provides business entities with a single point of contact for all the corporate dealings.

Disadvantages :

(a) Leads to concentration of risks. For instance, if a bank makes a substantial portion of loans to a single corporate entity and if it defaults, then the bank may land up in a serious trouble. The case of Punjab National Bank(PNB) and Nirav Modi proves the point.

(b) Lower interest spreads.

2. **Retail Banking :**
- In case of Retail banking, transactions are held directly with customers.
- Also referred to as 'Consumer banking', Retail banking is typical mass-market banking in which individual customers use local branches of larger commercial banks.
- Through the retail banking channel, financial services are provided to individuals and families.
- Here, no transactions take place with other banks or corporations.
- Through retail banking, all kinds of personal banking services are provided to the customer.
- These include:

(a) Deposit Services and related Transactions :
- Saving accounts, Fixed deposits and related transactions services such as Debit cards etc.

(b) Credit Services and Related Transactions :
- Personal loans, mortgages and related loans including Credit cards.

Advantages :
- Retail banking provides following advantages to banks:

(a) Large and loyal customer base.

(b) Diversified credit risks.

(c) Wide interest spreads.

(d) Profitability.

(e) Stability.

3. **Corporate Banking :**
- Also referred to as Business banking, 'Corporate banking' deals with corporate customers.

- Through this channel, loans are made to diverse business entities, ranging from small- to mid-sized local businesses large conglomerates.
- This loans support businesses to grow and hire people, thereby contributing to the development of the economy.
- Via Corporate banking, banks offer customized financial services to its corporate clientele, in the context of corporate financing and raising of capital.

Services of Corporate Banking :

- Various Corporate banking services include:

(a) Current account for business transactions.

(b) Credit management including loans and other credit products.

(c) Asset management.

(d) Cash management.

(e) Underwriting services.

(f) Treasury management services.

(g) Trade finance services such as Letter of credit, factoring, forfeiting.

(h) Employer services such as payroll and group retirement plans.

4. Investment Banking :

- Investment banking refers to a banking division which is engaged in creation of capital for corporates, governments and other entities.
- Through the Investment banking parlance, advice and management services for large, complex financial transactions are provided.
- An investment bank does not accept deposits.
- They are deal-makers between two or more large entities, and charge commission (or brokerage) on these deals.

Activities of the Investment Banking :

(a) Underwriting services for debt financing and the issuance of equity securities, as in an Initial Public Offering (IPO).

(b) Advising and facilitating Mergers and Acquisitions (M&As) for corporate entities, including Leveraged Buyouts (LBO's).

(c) Aid businesses, governments, and other large groups to plan and manage financial aspects of large projects.

(d) Offer ancillary services such as market making, trading of derivatives and equity securities.

5. Private Banking :

- Private banking refers to financial services provided by banks to HNI (High Net Worth) clients, who have enormous amounts of assets.
- Through Private banking, a wide range of wealth management services are provided under one roof.
- These financial services include banking, investment, tax management, insurance and allied services.
- Private banking even goes beyond to provide specialized services such as investment strategy and financial planning advice, portfolio management, customized financing options, retirement planning, and inheritance of wealth.
- With a primary focus on healthy individuals, a more intense, personal and tailor-made banking and investment services are made available to them
- Private banking is a stark contrast to retail banking, or mass banking.
- Existing products and services available in mass for retail banking are customized to meet the needs of HNI's.

Advantages :

(a) One-stop financial shop, with concierge services.

(b) Tailored proprietary solutions.

(c) Discounted or preferential pricing on products and services, such as prime interest rates on mortgages, or a favourable foreign exchange rate.

6. Development Banking :

- Also known as Term-lending institution or Development finance institution.
- Development Bank is principally a multi-purpose Financial Institution with a broad development outlook.

Definitions :

> **(a)** ***Diamond and Bosky :*** *Industrial finance and development corporations are 'development banks'.*
>
> **(b)** ***Business Dictionary :*** *"Development banks are financial institutions dedicated to fund new and upcoming businesses and economic development projects by providing equity capital and/or loan capital."*

- A development bank offers all types of financial assistance to business units, in the form of loans, underwriting, investment and guarantee operations, and promotional activities-economic development in general, and industrial development in particular.

- Initiated with the aim of increasing the pace of industrialization in the country, basic objective of a development bank is to promote economic development by encouraging investment and entrepreneurial activity.
- It encourages new and small entrepreneurs and seeks balanced regional growth.
- It provides long-term credit for capital-intensive investments spread over a long period and yielding low rates of return.
- Such investments are in the projects involving urban infrastructure, mining and heavy industry, and irrigation systems.
- Development banks usually, make availability of credit at low and stable rates of interest to promote long-term investments with considerable social benefits.
- In order to be able to lend for long-term, development banks require correspondingly long-term sources of finance, generally acquired by issuing long-dated securities in capital market, subscribed by long-term savings institutions such as pension funds, life insurance companies and post office deposits.
- Unlike commercial banks, a development bank does not accept deposits from the public.

Features of Development Bank :

(a)   It is a specialised financial institution, which offers medium and long-term finance to business units.

(b)   Unlike commercial banks, it does not accept deposits from the public.

(c)   It is a multi-purpose financial institution.

(d)   It provides financial assistance to the private sector as well as the public sector undertakings.

(e)   Its motive is to serve public interest ,with regards to development projects and entrepreneurship.

Some Development Banks in India:

(a)   Industrial Finance Corporation of India (IFCI).

(b)   State Finance Corporations (SFCs).

(c)   Small Industries Development Bank of India (SIDBI).

(d)   Export-Import (EXIM) Bank of India.

(e)   National Bank for Agriculture and Rural Development (NABARD).

Questions For Discussion :

1. Explain in detail the concept of a Bank.
2. Explain classification of banks in India
3. What is a Commercial bank ? State its types.
4. Explain in detail the concept of Co-operative bank.
5. Explain RRB.
6. Explain the concept of NBFC. How is it different from a bank?
7. Explain the difference between Commercial bank and Co-operative bank.
8. Explain Central bank alongwith its functions and objectives.

9. Write short notes on :

(A) Central banking.
(B) Co-operative banking.
(C) RRB.
(D) Development banking.
(E) Private banking.
(F) Retail banking.
(G) EXIM.
(H) NABARD.
(I) SIDBI.
(J) Wholesale banking.
(K) Scheduled bank.
(L) Differential banks.
(M) Payment banks.
(N) Small finance banks.
(O) Public sector banks.
(P) MUDRA.

Chapter **5**...

Concepts in Banking and Accounting of Transactions

Contents ...

Learning Objectives...

After studying this chapter, the student should understand:

1.   Accounting and financial statements of banks.

2.   Technology in Banking, Esp. Electronic banking.

3.   Concept of ATM.

4.   Concept of Internet Banking.

5.   Concept of Mobile banking/telephone banking.

6.   Concept of ECS (Electronic Clearing Service).

7.   Electronic Payment systems like RTGS,NEFT,EFT and IMPS.

8.   MICR, OCR, OMR, DATANET and Petty cash.

5.1 ACCOUNTING IN BANKS

- Just like other companies, accounting is a vital component of banks (or a banking company).
- Accounting is used within the banking environment to produce statutory accounts on an annual basis, or quarterly basis, mandated by the law.
- Just like other companies, financial accounting is used to prepare financial reports that provide information about the bank's performance to several stakeholders such as investors, creditors, tax authorities and auditors.
- Information contained in the financial reports help to reduce uncertainty in the minds of the users, regarding the financial position and performance of the bank.
- It helps answer questions concerning the profitability, availability of cash.

  Major Financial Statements of Banks :

- The major financial statements are designed to provide a picture of the overall financial position and performance of the bank.
- Through the financial statements, users get answer to questions such as the Financial reports are prepared according to Generally Accepted Accounting Principles (GAAP) guidelines.
- Financial reports of the bank mainly consist of the following Financial Statements prepared on a regular basis:
1. Income statement, or, The Profit and Loss Account.
2. Balance Sheet.
3. Cash Flow Statement.
- These financial statements help answer questions such as :
(a) How much profit was generated by the business over a particular period ?
(b) What is the accumulated wealth of the business at the end of a particular period ?
(c) What cash movements took place over a particular period ?
- The three statements are interrelated. The balance sheet reflects the combination of assets (including cash) and claims (including the owner's capital) of the business at a particular point in time.
- Both the Cash Flow Statement and the Profit and Loss Account explain the changes over a period of two of the items in the balance sheet, namely cash and owner's claim, respectively.

1. The Profit and Loss Account (Income Statement) :

- Also known as the income statement, profit and loss account (P&L) is to measure and report the profit generated by the bank over a period of time.
- Given below is the Format of Profit and Loss Account of SBI for FY 2019 :

State Bank of India :

- Profit and Loss Account for the year ended 31st March, 2019

Schedule No.		Year ended 31.03.2019 (Current Year) ₹	Year ended 31.03.2018 (Previous Year) ₹
I. INCOME			
Interest earned	13		
Other Income	14		
TOTAL			
II. EXPENDITURE			
Interest expended	15		
Operating expenses	16		
Provisions and contingencies			
TOTAL			
III. PROFIT			
Net Profit/(Loss) for the year			
Add: Profit/(Loss) brought forward			
Loss on amalgamation			
TOTAL			
IV. APPROPRIATIONS			
Transfer to Statutory Reserve			
Transfer to Capital Reserve			
Transfer to Revenue and other Reserves			
Balance carried over to Balance Sheet			
TOTAL			
Basic Earning per Share:			
Diluted Earning per Share:			
Significant Accounting Policies	17		
Notes to Accounts	18		

- Following are the major items of Profit & Loss Account :

(a) Income (Revenues) :

- It measures the inflow of assets, which arise as a result of banking operations.
- For example, sanctioning of loans to customers, fees for banking services such as lockers etc.
- The income of bank is different from a normal manufacturing or trading company.
- The income is further broken down into two heads:

(i) Interest Earned :

- The bank earns interest , mainly from the loans sanctioned to customers.
- Also, the bank gets interest from other banks and RBI.

(ii) Other Income /Fee Income :

- Also referred to as the Fee income or Non-interest income.
- Other income refers to fees and charges collected by the bank for the various banking services offered.
- Non-interest income comes from anything that does not constitute interest income.
- Several fees and charges are earned by the bank for services such as loan arrangement fees, annual credit card fee, locker fees, penalty etc.

(b) Interest Expended :

- The bank has to pay an interest to the depositors.
- Also, it has to pay interest to RBI and other banks if it has any borrowings from them.

(c) Provisions :

- It is an amount set aside out of profits to provide for anticipated losses arising from debts which may prove irrecoverable.
- These are, thus, similar to the accounts receivables and bad debt expense of a normal company.

2. Balance Sheet :

- Balance sheet shows the accumulated wealth of the bank at the end of a particular period.
- In other words, the balance sheet sets out the financial position of a business at a particular moment in time.

- The balance sheet reveals the forms in which the wealth of the business is held, and how much wealth is held in each form.
- It lists out the assets of the business on the one hand, and its liabilities on the other.
- A typical balance sheet consists of the core accounting equation, assets equal liabilities plus equity.

  | Assets = Capital + Liabilities |

- Given below is the Format of Balance sheet of SBI for FY 2019 :

State Bank of India

Balance Sheet as at 31st March, 2019

Schedule	As at 31.03.2019 (Current Year) ₹	As at 31.03.2018 (Previous Year) ₹
CAPITAL AND LIABILITIES		
Capital		
Reserves & Surplus		
Deposits		
Borrowings		
Other Liabilities and Provisions		
TOTAL		
ASSETS		
Cash and Balances with Reserve Bank of India		
Balances with Banks and Money at call and short notice		
Investments		
Advances		
Fixed Assets		
Other Assets		
TOTAL		
Contingent Liabilities		
Bills for Collection		
Significant Accounting Policies		
Notes to Accounts		

- Schedules referred to above form an integral part of the Balance Sheet.
- Following are the major items of Balance sheet of a bank:

(a) Loans / Advances as Assets :

- A bank's balance sheet is different from the company's balance sheet.
- As opposed to a company's balance sheet, in case of a bank, loans are recorded as assets.
- This is because the bank expects to receive interest and principal repayments for loans in the future, and thus generate economic benefit from the loans.
- A bank mainly advances loans to its corporate and retail clients.
- Loans form a major chunk of assets of the bank, because main operations and source of revenue for banks are their loan and deposit operations.

(b) Deposits as Liabilities :

- In case of a bank, 'Deposits' are recorded as liabilities, because this is the amount of money the bank owes to its depositors.
- Deposits are expected to be withdrawn by customers or also pay out interest payments, generating an economic outflow in the future.

(c) Provisions :

- The bank must be prepared in the event that borrowers are not able to pay-off their loans.
- These bad pieces of credit are written-off in the income statement as a provision for credit loss.

(d) Capital :

- Also referred to as Owners 'Equity or Shareholders' funds.
- Capital represents the claim of owners against the business.

(3) The Cash Flow Statement :

- The cash flow statement is a summary of the cash receipts and payments over the period of reporting.
- In other words, cash movements that took place over a particular period are depicted in the cash flow statement.
- All payments of a particular type are added together to give just one figure which appears in the statement.
- The net total of the statement is the net increase or decrease of the cash in the bank over the period.

- As with other companies, the Cash flow statement is classified into:
(a) Cash flow from Operating activities,
(b) Cash flow from Investing activities,
(c) Cash flow from Financing activities.

Bank's Debits and Credits :

- Whenever the message from the bank reads "Your account has been credited, "it means there is an increase of balance (money) in your account.

- Conversely, when the message from the bank reads "Your account has been debited", it means there is a   decrease of balance (money) from your account.

- Thus, the 'Debit' and 'Credit' terminologies as regards of bank account is different from conventional accounting, wherein debiting the Cash account in the general ledger increases its balance and crediting the Cash account in the general ledger reduces its balance.

5.2 ELECTRONIC BANKING

Definition :

> *"Electronic Banking is the use of a computer to retrieve and process banking data and to initiate transactions directly with a bank via a tele-communications network."*
> **- Lipis et al, 1986.**

- Nowadays, brick and mortar branches are being aided(as well as replaced in some cases)due to technological advancements in the banking sector.

- Information technology has been important in terms of transactions processing as well as for various other internal systems and processes.

- The various technological platforms used by banks for the conduct of their day to day operations, their manner of reporting and the way in which interbank transactions and clearing is affected has evolved substantially over the years.

- Computerisation, which started with installation of simple computers to automate the functioning of branches marked the beginning of all technological initiatives in the banking industry.

- There has been increasing importance of total banking automation in the Indian Banking Industry.

- Now, Indian banks have become computerized with CBS (Core Banking Solutions), and technology enabled with a host of products like ATM, Internet banking and Mobile banking.

- Thus, Indian banking system has evolved to play a vital role in economic development of the country.
- Banking system in the country has transformed to provide excellent technology oriented customer service and from Class banking to Mass banking.
- Technology developments in financial sector have improved customer service largely (both in terms of time and cost).
- The Government also looks to prevent the circulation of cryp to currencies and to exploit the use of block chain technology proactively for ushering in digital economy.

1. **Core Banking Solution (CBS):**

- Core banking solutions refer to an array of services provided by a group of networked bank branches.
- CORE stands for "Centralized Online Real-time Environment".
- Core Banking Solution (CBS) is networking of branches, which enables Customers to operate their accounts, and avail banking services from any branch of the Bank on CBS network, regardless of where the account is maintained by him.
- As a result, the customer is no more the customer of a Branch, but he becomes the Bank's Customer.
- Thus CBS is in short, a step towards enhancing customer convenience through 'Anywhere and Anytime Banking'.

Benefits of CBS Technology :

(a) Reduction of operation costs.
(b) Faster and enhanced customer service.
(c) Integration of banking products and services, leading to improved risk management.
(d) Mitigation of Operational Risk.
(e) Real-time transaction processing.
(f) Efficient and easy transactions.
(g) 24/7 availability.
(h) Anywhere anytime Banking.

5.3 ATM

- ATM (Automated Teller Machine) has been the most popular banking technology in India.

- Through ATM card, customers can complete basic banking transactions without the assistance of a branch representative or teller through ATM machines (electronic bank outlets).

Definition :

> *"The Automated Teller Machine (ATM) is an automatic banking machine which allows banks customers to process account transactions."*

- The first ATM appeared in London in 1967, and in less than 50 years, ATMs have their presence all around the world, form a major country to even tiny little island nations.
- ATM is basically a card issued by a bank that can be used at an ATM for deposits, withdrawals , account information or other kind of transactions , often through interbank networks.
- It is operated by plastic card with its special features and is replacing cheque and personal attendance of the customer.
- ATM's enables the customers to withdraw their money 24 hours a day 7 days a week.
- ATM machine authenticates the customer with a Personal Identification Number (PIN), which must match the PIN stored in the chip on the card, or in the issuing financial institution's database.
- In addition to that, ATMs can also be used for payment of utility bills, funds transfer between accounts, balance enquiry, deposit of cheques and cash into accounts etc.
- ATMs can also be used to withdraw cash (foreign currency) in a foreign country.

Advantages :

1. ATMs are a convenient way to manage money.
2. Accessibility, considering huge number of ATM machines.
3. 24*7 banking transactions available.
4. Saves time for the customers.
5. For the banks, ATM's enable them to provide seamless customer service without actually opening a brick and mortar branch.
6. Less expensive than using a cheque cashing service.

Types of ATM :

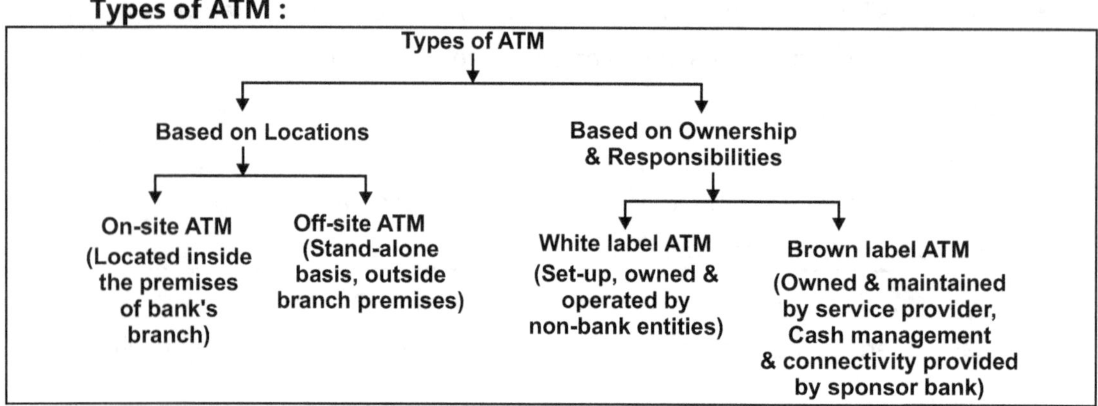

Fig. 5.1 : Types of ATMs

(I)   Depending upon Location :

1.   On-site ATM :

- On-site ATM's are located inside the premises of a Bank's branch.
- As a result, customers have the option of using, both the physical branch and the ATM .
- Bank customers can make use of On-site ATM to avoid long queues in the branch and hence save on the time required to complete their transactions.

2.   Off-site ATM :

- Off-site ATM's are set-up on a standalone basis.
- They are located outside the bank premises.
- They are usually located at other places, such as shopping centres, airports, railways station and petrol stations.
- Off-site ATM's are launched to ensure that the bank reaches out to more geographical areas and that people are able to use the banking services, even when there is no bank branch in the area.

(II)   Depending upon Ownership and Responsibilities :

1.   White Label ATM :

- White Label ATMs refer to the ATMs which are set-up, owned and operated by non-bank entities such as NBFC's.
- RBI had allowed private non-bank establishments to set-up, own and operate its own brand of ATMs in the country in order to aid financial inclusion and drive ATM penetration in the country.
- White Labelled ATMs (WLAs) will not display logo of any particular bank.

- The first white label ATM in India was launched by TATA under the brand name 'Indicash'.

2. **Brown Label ATM :**

- Brown Label ATM's are owned and maintained by a service provider.
- However, cash management and connectivity to banking networks is provided by a sponsor bank (whose brand is used on ATM).

5.4 INTERNET BANKING

- This system allows individuals to perform banking activities at home, through the internet.
- Internet Banking allows a customer to conduct bank transactions online, instead of finding a bank and interacting with a teller.
- It is a means to transfer funds directly from one account to another, rather than by cheque or cash.
- Through Internet banking, customers can view their account details, pay bills, and transfer money by means of the internet.

Definition :

> *"Internet banking implies a service that allows the customer to conduct the financial transactions electronically, with the use of Internet."*

Advantages:

1. The facility is simple to open and easy to operate.
2. Convenient for transfer of funds and payment of bills.
3. No need for the customer to keep receipts of his bills, as he can easily view his transactions.
4. All time availability, and the customer can perform his tasks from anywhere and at any time, even at night or on holidays when the bank is closed.
5. No need for the customer to stand in long queue to pay-off his bills.
6. Fast and efficient service.
7. Even additional financial services such as loans and investment options are available for the customer through the Internet banking platform.
8. Banks can use Internet banking as a medium to endorse their financial products.

Disadvantages :

1. Active Internet connection is essential.

2. Understanding usage of Internet may be difficult for senior citizens.
3. If password gets stolen or compromised, security threat may arise.
4. If the bank's server is down, the customer cannot access his accounts , and make transactions.
5. Constant messages and updates can lead to annoying the customer.

5.5 MOBILE BANKING / TELEPHONE BANKING

Definition :

"Mobile banking refers to the service provided by a bank or other financial institution, through which customers can conduct financial transactions remotely using a mobile device such as a smartphone or tablet."

- Through mobile banking, entire non-cash related banking can be done on telephone /mobile.
- Unlike the related internet banking, mobile banking uses software (known as app), provided by the financial institution for the banking transactions.
- Mobile banking continues to be a focus area for all banks in India as mobile penetration is high amongst Indians nowadays.
- Banks are looking at this channel as a way to increase their customer engagement in urban and to reach out to new ones in rural regions

Services provided by Mobile banking app:
1. Balance enquiry.
2. List of latest transactions as well as Account statement.
3. Electronic Bill Payments.
4. Remote Check Deposits.
5. P2P payments.
6. Funds transfers between a customer's or another's accounts.
7. Branch locator and ATM locator.
8. Requests for a cheque book, new debit card, credit card, duplicate debit card, etc.

Advantages :
1. Ease of use.
2. Speed.
3. Flexibility.
4. Convenient way to access accounts and make payments including bills.

5. Personalization with features such as Preferred Language, default transactions, Ms-alerts, format regarding time, date and amount etc.

6. Enhanced security with tools such as One Time Password (OTPs).

7. For the bank, it provides cost reduction. The cost of handling transactions decrease with the diminished need of customers to visit the bank branch.

5.6 ECS (ELECTRONIC CLEARING SERVICE)

Definition :

> *"ECS refers to an electronic mode of transfer of funds from one bank account to another bank account."*

- ECS enables electronic credit/debit transaction associated with customer's account.
- In other words, ECS system can be used for both credit and debit purposes.
- ECS is generally used for repetitive and periodic transactions.
- Monthly/ quarterly/ half-yearly/ yearly payments can be done through ECS.
- Institutions such as Banks, Corporations, Government departments make use of ECS for payments such as interest, salary, pension, commission, dividends etc.
- ECS can also be used by individuals and families to make bill payments for utilities such as telephone, electricity, water, and even for making Equated Monthly Instalments (EMI) payments on loans and for making SIP investments
- ECS obviates the need for issuing and handling paper instruments and thereby facilitates improved customer service by the Banks and Companies/ Corporations/ Government Departments effecting bulk payments.
- For availing the ECS service, the customer must inform his bank and provide a mandate that authorises the institution, who can then debit or credit the payments through the bank

Types of ECS :

- Basically, there are two types of ECS, viz;

1. ECS (Credit),
2. ECS (Debit).

1. ECS (Credit) :

- ECS (Credit) is used for making credit to a large number of beneficiaries by raising a single debit to an account.

Example: Dividend payments, Interest payment, Salary payment.

2. ECS (Debit) :

- ECS (Debit) is used for raising debits to a number of accounts of consumers/ account holders for crediting a particular institution.

  Advantages:

(a) Reduced paper handling, and hence, environment-friendly.

(b) The end beneficiary (i.e. the customer) is not required to make frequent visits to his bank for depositing the physical paper instruments.

(c) Faster and transparent process.

5.7 ELECTRONIC PAYMENT SYSTEMS (RTGS,NEFT,EFT,IMPS)

- Banks provide facilities for the transfer of money to any place within and out of the country.

- The funds are transferred by means of draft, telephonic transfer, electronic transfer such as internet banking, RTGS, NEFT etc.

- In the last decade, India has seen a shift from traditional payment methods, i.e., cash/paper-based payments to modern electronic payment systems.

- Systems such as EFT, RTGS, NEFT have been used.

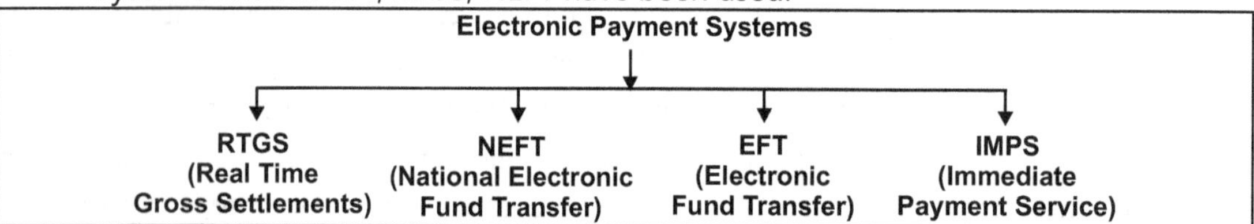

Fig. 5.2 : Electronic Payment Systems

1. Real Time Gross Settlement (RTGS):

- RTGS was introduced in India since March 2004.

- As the name indicates, this system runs on 'Real Time basis'.

- Real-time gross settlement is usually employed for large-value interbank funds transfers.

- RTGS enables electronic transfer of funds on a gross and real-time settlement basis.

- Gross means continuous or real-time settlement of fund transfers individually on an order by order basis, without netting.

- 'Real Time' means the processing of instructions at the time funds are received (immediately).

- Through this system, electronics instructions can be given by banks to transfer funds from their account to the account of another bank.
- RTGS system is primarily meant for large value transactions that require and receive immediate clearing.
- This system is maintained and operated by the RBI and provides a means of efficient and speedy transfer of funds amongst banks.
- As the settlement of funds takes place in the books of the Reserve Bank of India, the payments are final and irrevocable.
- The minimum amount to be transferred through RTGS is ₹ 2 lakh and there is no upper limit on RTGS transactions.

Information Needed for Initiating RTGS by the Bank :

- The customer making remittance of funds must furnish the following information to a bank for initiating a RTGS transaction:

(a) Amount to be transferred.

(b) The account number to be debited.

(c) Name of the beneficiary bank and branch.

(d) The IFSC number of the receiving branch.

(e) Name of the beneficiary customer.

(f) Account number of the beneficiary customer.

(g) Sender to receiver information, if any.

Advantages of RTGS :

(a) Safety :

- RTGS is a safe and secure system for funds transfer.

(b) Huge Amounts :

- RTGS transactions have no upper limit on the amount that can be transferred.

(c) Availability :

- RTGS system is available on all days when most bank branches are functioning (including Saturdays).

(d) Real Time Transfer :

- There is real time transfer of funds to the beneficiary account.

(e) No Physical Documents Required :

- The remitter need not use a physical cheque or a demand draft.

(f) Beneficiary :

- The beneficiary of the funds need not be worried about loss or theft of physical instruments or the likelihood of fraudulent encashment thereof.

(g) No Visit to Branch Required :

- The customer remitting the funds can initiate the remittances from his home / place of work using internet banking, if the bank offers such service.
- Moreover, the beneficiary need not visit a bank branch for depositing the paper instruments

(h) Low Transaction Charges :

- Transaction charges are low, as RBI has imposed a cap on the same.

(i) Legal Support :

- The transaction has legal backing of the county's monetary authority.

(j) Elimination of Settlement Risk :

- With RTGS transaction, settlement risk or delivery risk gets eliminated, as interbank settlement usually occurs in real time throughout the day.

RTGS Payment Process :

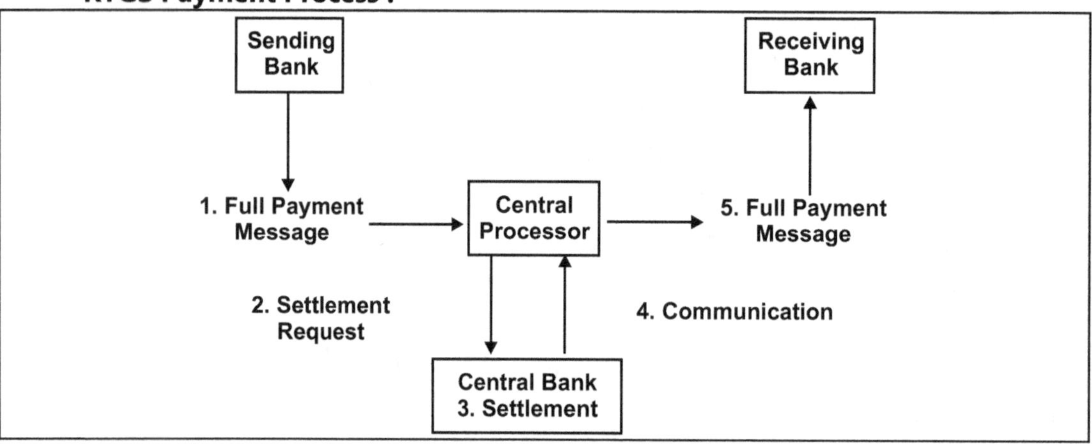

Fig. 5.3 : RTGS Payment Process

2. NEFT (National Electronic Funds Transfer) :

Definition :

> *"NEFT is an electronic nation-wide, Inter Bank Transfer mechanism, facilitating one-to-one funds transfer."*

- Through NEFT, individuals and businesses can electronically transfer funds from any bank branch to any individual or business entity having an account with any other bank branch in the country participating in this Scheme of Payment system.

- Under NEFT, the settlement takes place in batches, that are settled in hourly time slots.
- To understand in simple terms, if an individual wishes to transfer a sum of money from his bank account to another person's bank account, he can make use of NEFT process, instead of withdrawing money and then paying it in cash or by writing out a cheque
- With an increased emphasis on online banking, NEFT has become one of the most common ways of transferring funds.
- NEFT service is not restricted to personal fund transfers alone, and can also be used to make payments for loans, EMI's, credit cards dues and more.

Advantages:

(a) Charges :

- NEFT transaction initiated through online channels such as internet banking, and certain mobile apps is Nil.
- Even transaction charges for NEFT transactions through bank branch channel are very low.

(b) Convenience :

- Since a bank customer can transfer funds electronically, from any bank branch to any individual, it has eliminated the need to visit a bank branch for transfer of funds.

Difference between NEFT and RTGS:

Basis	NEFT	RTGS
(a) Basic Operation :	NEFT operates on a deferred settlement basis, and fund transfer is settled in batches.	Under RTGS, the funds transfer takes place on a real time basis. It means that the transfer of funds take place at the time the request is received.
(b) Minimum Amount :	No minimum amount for funds remitted through NEFT.	The minimum amount for funds remitted through RTGS is ₹ 2 lakh.
(c) Suitability :	Small value transactions.	High value transactions.

Basis	NEFT	RTGS
(d) Processing Speed :	Comparatively slower as compared to RTGS.	Fast.
(e) Transfer Charges :	For transfers up to ₹ 10,000 - ₹ 2.50 per transaction. For transfers of ₹ 10,000 to ₹ 1 lakh → ₹ 5 For ₹ 1 lakh to ₹ 2 lakh → up to ₹ 15 For transfer above ₹ 2 lakh → up to ₹ 25	For transactions of ₹ 2 lakh to ₹ 5 lakh → ₹ 25-30 Transactions above ₹ 5 lakh – ₹ 50-55

3. **EFT (Electronic Funds Transfer) :**
- EFT refers to the electronic transfer of money from one bank account to another.
- This transfer can either be, within a single financial institution, or across multiple institutions.
- The transfers happen through computer-based systems, without the direct intervention of bank staff.
- EFT transactions are called electronic cheques or e-cheques also.
- Nowadays, internet-based EFT is widely used, wherein a customer logs in to the bank's website and registers another bank account. He then places a request to transfer certain amount to that account. If this account is in the same bank, customer's bank transfers the amount to this account.
- If this account is in another bank, the transfer request is forwarded to an ACH (Automated Clearing House) to transfer the amount to other account and the amount is deducted from the customer's account.
- Once the amount is transferred to other account, the customer is notified of the fund transfer by the bank.

4. **IMPS (Immediate Payment Service) :**
- Initiated in 2010,the money transfer mechanism of IMPS was made available by the Central bank of the country, the Reserve Bank of India (RBI) and the National Payments Corporation of India (NPCI).
- IMPS refers to an instant interbank electronic fund transfer service through mobile phones. It is also being extended through other channels such as ATM, Internet Banking, etc.

- IMPS offers robust & real time fund transfer which offers an instant, 24X7, interbank electronic fund transfer service that can be   accessed on multiple channels like Mobile, Internet, ATM, SMS, and Branch.
- IMPS transactions are convenient and instant, and requires only the below information to be furnished to effect an IMPS remittance from Person to Person.
- MMID of the beneficiary (seven digit number of which the first four digits are the unique identification number of the bank offering IMPS).
- Mobile number of the beneficiary.
- Name of the beneficiary.

Necessary Details for IMPS Remittance :

- In order to effect an IMPS remittance from Person to Account, following details are required:

(a) Name of the beneficiary,

(b) Account Number of the beneficiary,

(c) IFS Code of the beneficiary bank.

- After the customer's account is debited and funds have been credited in the beneficiary's account, the remitting bank sends a confirmation message to the remitting customer about the transaction initiated by him.
- Likewise, even the beneficiary bank sends a confirmation message to the beneficiary customer informing him regarding the credit of funds in his account.
- IMPS mechanism is regulated by RBI and is managed by National Payments Corporation of India (NPCI).
- IMPS is slated to be a precursor in electronification of retail payments in the country

Advantages:

(a) 24*7 *365 service and hence, scores over National Electronic Fund Transfer (NEFT) and RTGS (Real-time Gross Settlement) transfer mechanisms which are only available during banking hours.

(b) Convenient service as the transaction can be done using only the mobile number and MMID of the beneficiary.

(c) Instant transfer of funds to the beneficiary.

(d) IMPS service is economical, as banks usually levy very nominal charges for remitting money through IMPS.

Comparison of NEFT, RTGS and IMPS :

Point of Difference	NEFT	RTGS	IMPS
1. Minimum Transfer Value :	₹ 1.	₹ 2 lakhs	₹ 1
2. Payment Options :	Online and Offline	Online and Offline	Online
3. Maximum Transfer Value :	No limit	No limit	₹ 2 lakhs
4. Settlement Type :	Half hourly basis	Real time	Real time
5. Service Timings :	8 a.m. – 7 p.m. (working days)	8 a.m. – 6 p.m. (working days	Available 365 days 24 × 7
6. Inward Transaction Charges :	No charges	No charges	Decided by the individual member banks and PPIs

5.8. MICR (Magnetic Ink Character Recognition)

Definition :

> *"Magnetic Ink Character Recognition (MICR) is a 9-digit code that uniquely identifies a particular bank branch participating in the Electronic Clearing System (ECS)."*

- MICR code is a code printed on cheques using MICR (Magnetic Ink Character Recognition technology) for enabling identification of the cheques resulting in faster processing.
- Magnetic ink character recognition line is printed using technology that allows certain computers to read and process the printed information.

- MICR code can be found on the bottom of a cheque leaf, next to the cheque number, as well as on the first page of a bank savings account passbook.
- The 9 –digit MICR code comprises of 3 parts as below :
- First three digits represent the city (aligned with PIN code).
- Next 3 digits represent the bank (Bank Code).
- Last 3 digits represent the branch (Branch Code).

   Advantages :

1. Rapidly facilitates routing information.
2. MICR technology makes it difficult to alter cheques.
3. Faster clearing of cheques.

5.9 OCR, OMR AND DATANET

1. **OCR (Optical Character Recognition) :**

- Optical character recognition (OCR) is a software that identifies and retrives text from documents and images, allowing them to be understood and processed by a computer.
- In other words, OCR converts scanned documents in a system, to machine readable text document.
- OCR is a technology that recognizes text within a digital image.
- The banking industry was amongst the first users of OCR.
- OCR has revolutionized banking industry, making banking transactions faster.
- OCR has facilitated processing of cheques due to their ability to read the cheque numbers printed at the bottom.
- Using a scanner and OCR, bank passbooks can be scanned and updated with the last entry.
- In addition to reading the cheque number, account number and the amount, OCR in banks is able to scan and decipher the signatures on the cheques as well.

Advantages :

(a) Speedier transaction.

(b) Reduction in errors as a result of minimum human intervention.

(c) Standardizes the operation of each department, and simplifies the processes.

(d) Optimize business costs.

(e) With digitizing documents , OCR helps the bank save the necessary storage space for the same information, decreasing it from a few square meters to only a few bytes on the computer.

(f) Reduced use of paper helps protect the environment.

2. OMR (Optical Mark Recognition) :

- OMR refers to the process of automatically extracting data from noticeable fields, such as cheque-boxes and fill-in the fields, on printed forms.

Definition :

> *"Optimal Mark Recognition (OMR) is an electronic method of gathering human-handled data by identifying certain markings on a documents."*

- In banking industry, OMR process can be used as a supplement to OCR

3. DataNet :

- Using secure DataNet, a bank customer   can access his account anytime, anywhere.

- Several banking services like checking account balance, viewing transaction history, or payment of bills can be executed in a matter of minute.

DataNet Services :

(a) Viewing account balance.

(b) Review transaction history.

(c) Make transfers.

(d) Payment of bills.

(e) View images and print copies of paid cheques.

(f) Download account history.

(g) Order cheque books.

(h) Stop payment instructions

(i)   Receive e-mail alerts for new messages, balance thresholds, and transactions.

(j)   Opening of a new account.

(k)   Applying for a loan.

5.10 PETTY CASH

- Also referred to as the Petty Cash Fund.
- Petty cash is small amount of cash on hand , available for paying small expenses without writing a cheque.
- The petty cash is controlled through the use of a petty cash voucher for each payment made.
- The expenses for petty cash will be recorded in the company's General Ledger Expense Accounts, when the petty cash on hand is replenished.
- Petty cash can be used for small day-to-day expenses such as office supplies, stationery, reimbursing employees for expenses etc.
- Though a small amount, companies employ strict internal controls to manage the petty cash fund.
- When a petty cash fund is in use, petty cash transactions are still recorded on financial statements.
- No accounting journal entries are made when purchases are made using petty cash.
- However, when the custodian needs more cash, or when he receives new funds in exchange for the receipts, the journal entries are recorded.
- The journal entry for giving the custodian more cash is a debit to the Petty Cash Fund and a credit to Cash Account.

Examples of Petty Cash Payments:

1.   Paying the courier ₹ 40 for the postage due on a letter.

2.   Reimbursing an employee for ₹ 120 for supplies purchased.

3.   Reimbursing an employee for purchasing ₹ 50 for snacks for an early morning meeting.

Questions For Discussion :

1. Explain in detail the accounting and financial statements in a Bank.

2. Explain different Electronic payment systems.

3. What do you mean by Electronic banking ? How has technology benefitted the Banking industry ?

4. Explain the concept of ATM. State its different types.

5. **Write short notes on :**

(A)   NEFT.

(B)   RTGS.

(C)   ECS.

(D)   IMPS.

(E)   Petty Cash.

(F)   DATANET.

(G)   OCR and OMR.

(H)   MICR.

(I)   CBS.

(J)   Mobile banking.

(K)   Internet banking.

(L)   EFT.

FINANCIAL MARKETS AND BANKING OPERATIONS

(M.B.A. : Semester – II)
(New 2019 Pattern)

Time : 2 ½ Hours   **Maximum Marks : 50**

Instructions to the candidates :

    (i) Attempt All Questions.

    (ii) Figures to the right indicate full marks.

Q. 1 : Explain the Role of Financial System in Economic Development.   **[10]**

OR

Q. 1 : Explain the various Players in Indian Money Market.   **[10]**

Q. 2 : Describe the various Capital Market Instruments.   **[10]**

OR

Q. 2 (a) What is Crypto-currency Market ?   **[5]**

  (b) What is Primary and Secondary Market ?   **[5]**

Q. 3 : Explain the various Types of Banks.   **[10]**

OR

Q. 3 : Explain the various Types of NBFCs.   **[10]**

Q. 4 : What is Internet Banking ? State its Advantages and Disadvantages.   **[10]**

OR

Q. 4 (a) What is Electronic Clearing Service ?   **[5]**

  (b) What is Optical Character Recognition (OCR) ?   **[5]**

Q. 5 : **Write Short Notes (Attempt any two) :**   **[10]**

  (A) Futures and Options.

  (B) Role of Central Bank in Money Market.

  (C) Role of SEBI in Capital Market.

  (D) RTGS and NEFT.

(M. 1)

M.B.A. : Semester – II

(Compulsory Generic Core Course)

- **Marketing Management**
- **Human Resource Management**
- **Financial Management**
- **Operations & Supply Chain Management**